Tattoo
Behind the Needle

Joy Surles

Published by:

PO Box 223 • Stillwater, MN 55082
www.wolfpub.com

Legals

First published in 2009 by Wolfgang Publications Inc.,
PO Box 223, Stillwater MN 55082

The information in this book is true and complete to the best of our
knowledge. All recommendations are made without any guarantee on
the part of the author or publisher, who also disclaim any liability
incurred in connection with the use of this data or specific details.

We recognize that some words, model names and designations, for
example, mentioned herein are the property of the trademark holder.
We use them for identification purposes only. This is not an official
publication.

ISBN number: 1-929133-78-2
ISBN-13: 978-1-929133-78-9

Printed and bound in China.

Tattoo Behind The Needle

Acknowledgements

I'd like to thank each of the artists who shared their work with me and who took the time to answer my endless stream of questions. I'm honored to have had the opportunity to write about each of you.

Introduction

THE STATE OF THE ART TODAY

In choosing the tattooists to interview for this book, I compiled a list of the artists whom I believed represented the bleeding edge of what is possible in tattoo art today. From Brandon Bond's Atlanta tattoo oligarchy to the smaller, one-man shows such as John Wayne and Matt Griffith, the artists whose works appear in the following pages are all pioneers, pushing the boundaries and breaking the rules, updating the ancient, indelible art for the 21st Century.

While conducting the interviews, certain themes emerged as the artists told their individual stories and explained theories behind their artistry. In many ways, these themes represent a kind of recipe for what makes a tattooist great. For instance, each artist considers him or herself to be something of an outsider in the industry; however, they all express great respect for their predecessors, and they suggest that breaking the rules is only possible when you know those rules well. They all mentioned the difficulty in striking a balance between protecting their artistic integrity and recognizing that it is their job as tattooists to create art that will please their clients. They all spoke well of the tattoo industry and the changes that have revolutionized it in the last few decades, and each has shown a unique method of harnessing the energy in these changes to invigorate the creative spirit driving tattoo art. For artists just starting out in the industry or looking to add a new spark to their creative practice, these ideas might serve as a guide for how to develop a great career.

Furthermore, other themes that arose in these discussions highlighted many of the most significant changes in the tattoo world over the last several years. Again and again, the word "Renaissance" came up as each artist described his or her first-hand observations of the level of talent and artistic achievement that has rocked the tattoo world in recent years. While the art itself has certainly become more acceptable in pop culture through reality television, adaptation of traditional artwork in clothing and other merchandise, and the increasing presence of tattoo artwork on celebrities other than the rock gods who inspired many of us to first explore the art, these artists speak about much more than popularity when they refer to the "Renaissance." From the breathtaking realism that marks such artists as Joshua Carlton and Dan Henk to the abstract expressionism of Amanda Wachob, the tattoo industry has been infused with new life from these and others.

The career of "tattooist" is becoming recognized as a respectable profession, and many of the artists commented on the influx of art school graduates at the street shops. As graphic design, illustration, and other more traditional means of employment for creative types became more competitive and the demand for high-quality tattoo art has grown, tattooing has become an attractive option for artists seeking a way to make their living through art. It has lead to a true tattoo revolution, with new styles developing, new techniques emerging, and new names grabbing the headlines in the tattoo media.

While much has changed, as much has remained the same. Young artists such as Sunny Buick, Chris Thomas, and Sean Herman continue to use traditional tattoo imagery and techniques, albeit updated with new subject matter and hybridized with more modern color schemes and other styles. Tattoo art still tends toward the darker side, with the hyperrealists frequently turning to the imagery of horror films in their pursuit of the next perfect image for a high-impact piece. Artists like Shannon Schober continue to put the wearer's interests firsts in aspects of design, such as placement on the body to highlight the wearer's unique musculature and curves. And nearly every artist has a story of a favorite client, a favorite piece, or a wild night at a convention, underscoring the idea that no matter how mainstream tattoos may become, tattoo people are still *different*.

If you've picked up this book, then you are one of those different folks. I hope you enjoy taking a first-hand look behind the needles of some of the greatest artists working today.

Chapter One

Brandon Bond

Color Master and Business Mastermind

"Oh my God! I am so glad to meet you! It's an honor! It's really an honor," gushed an enthusiast at the 2006 North Carolina tattoo convention. The crowd was thick around the All or Nothing booth. Brandon Bond shook his fan's hand, but he seemed a little put off by the attention. "I thought he was going to bow to me or something," he said. The combination of Brandon's charismatic, balls-out personality, his unparalleled talent for color, and his enthusiastic embrace of the evolution of tattoo culture has created a kind of social juggernaut. He is one of the best-known artists in the industry today, and his zeal is contagious. His appearances at conventions are increasingly rare, but when he shows

Brandon Bond is a talented tattooist who tirelessly promotes many business interests. Despite the demands of his businesses, Brandon continues to practice the tattooist's art.

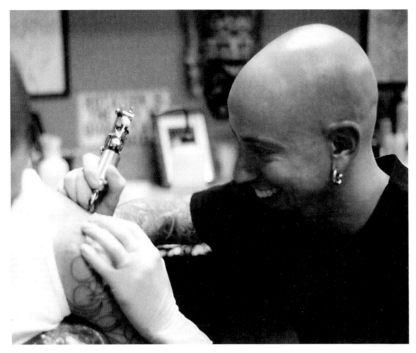

Although he has virtually eliminated his touring, Brandon continues to work in his Atlanta studios.

and a bad businessman, or a great businessman and a terrible artist. Or even worse, the studio is owned by someone who is not a tattoo artist at all…that never works…at least not for the artists anyway."

In his self-published memoir Whore, which combines autobiography with art and serves as Brandon's statement of his artistic philosophy, he explains his goals in opening his shops, "I wake up every morning with a list of shit I have to get done exploding in my head…The last thing on my list was to open a studio unlike any other, and I think we have accomplished that…I made a decision years ago that if tattooing was all I was going to do, I was going to do it as hard

up, the crowds follow. The tattoo cognoscenti have embraced Brandon as one of the leaders of the present generation of tattooing.

His Empire

After years of touring the tattoo convention circuit, Brandon settled in Atlanta, Georgia, before creating one of the United States' most exciting tattoo empires. Atlanta is among the fastest growing cities in the nation. This high-energy environment has fostered the growth of Brandon's tattoo enterprise, attracting world-class artists and sophisticated clientele. Atlanta has long been known as a tattoo town, and if Brandon Bond has his way, it will become the heart of tattoo culture. His two studios, All or Nothing—which, although it stays booked for months in advance, has the vibe of a street shop—and A.N.T.I. Art Elite, his luxurious, spa-quality private studio, are two of the busiest tattoo studios in the world.

Brandon has created a successful triangulation in his tattoo enterprise; he and the artists he hires all create world-class tattoo art, he is a consummate businessman, and his shops are known for providing excellent customer service. According to Bond, "In a lot of studios, the owner is either a great artist

Brandon Bond

Notice the brilliant blues …

…and the sense of movement …

…in this sleeve that clearly expresses Brandon Bond's signature style.

and as fast as I could…I have not wasted time in years. It is the most valuable commodity on the planet."

HIS STYLE

Brandon developed a reputation for being a master colorist early in his career. In the many years he spent on the road, he was careful to land in towns with artists who could contribute to the development of his signature style. He'd scan through the tattoo magazines, find an artist he admired, go to that artist and get a tattoo. For the cost of a tattoo, he'd also get an education from some of the best in the industry.

He credits Joe Capobianco as being one of his early influences, and there are traces of Capobianco in the impressive color work that marks Brandon's best pieces.

The hyper-color, high-impact style that Brandon's All or Nothing crew has adapted and expanded has become the standard that the industry meets, and Brandon himself is on the forefront of this movement. From a sense of dynamic movement to the illusion of depth that he achieves, Brandon is truly one of the industry's best.

In the blue geisha and gold Buddha sleeve pictured here, for instance, we see many of the trademark techniques that have contributed to Brandon's reputation in the industry. Brandon uses his signature blue palette, ranging from deep jewel tones to near-white, to achieve a haunting, hyper-realistic effect in many of his pieces. The blue faces in the upper part of the sleeve highlight the menacing tone, suggesting a beautiful, but angry, death.

He juxtaposes the anger and sadness apparent in the zombie geishas gracefully with the serene Buddha and lotus flower on the bottom half of the sleeve, where the theme shifts from darkness to light—from menace to transcendence. Notice the delicate shading in the Buddha's face, the three-dimensional appearance of contour in the cheekbones and eye sockets, and the brilliant golds that appear almost to have been lit from within.

Another characteristic effect that Brandon has included in this sleeve is a sense of movement. The top-most geisha's hair blows in the wind, and the greywash, swirling background—combining solid black whirls with those rendered through negative space—contribute to the sense of movement in the piece. This motion guides the viewer's eye through the emotional transformation that takes place in the sleeve, from the rage in the top Geisha's red-lit eyes to the sadness and shock on the second blue face, and finally down to the uplifting image of the Buddha and the lotus, which achieve a quality of peace and light in the midst of such darkness. The slightly uplifted petals of the lotus flower, which support and surround the Buddha's face, tie the image together in terms of theme, color, and movement.

While many artists use one or more of these effects in their tattoos, Brandon is unique in his dynamic use of all of them and the graceful union of order through the chaos.

Another effect that has become increasingly common in Brandon's work in recent years is his combination of intense realism with fantastic elements, as in this interpretation of Medusa. The skin tones in Medusa's face and hand, the realistic contours in her face, the textural effects of scaling on the snakes, and the illusion of three dimensions in the striking snake's mouth and appearance of perspective in the foreground of the image all enhance the mythic theme by making the impossible seem achievable. While fantasy and myth have long been common themes in tattoo artwork, Brandon interprets these images in a manner as to make them seem real, or hyper-real, which can create some disconcerting effects for the viewer.

He accomplishes a similar sense of depth to that in the snake's mouth in his Labyrinth piece. The grades in shading from soft pinks through deep, rich reds, to the black in the cavernous mouth, especially behind the frame of the yellowish-white teeth, create a spectacular illusion of three-dimensions.

HIS BUSINESS

Brandon threatens to retire, periodically, and the frantic pace he maintains while running his businesses, promoting his artists, and creating new tattoos keeps him in a perpetual state of chaos. In Whore, he explained that if he spoke for just 15 minutes a day with all of his staff, "that is seven and a half hours of time eaten up. I don't think they even realize that. When you add clients, advertisers, supply people, and emails to the mix, you have a 14-hour workday. That is without me doing any-

The combination of realism with fantasy creates a striking piece in this three-panel view of Brandon's "Medusa."

Brandon Bond achieves the impression of depth in this Labyrinth piece through masterful shading.

Here is a beautiful sleeve that features realistic flesh tones instead of Brandon's famous blues.

9

This half sleeve features a high-contrast portrait.

This Golden Buddha is an alternative take on one of Bond's favorites.

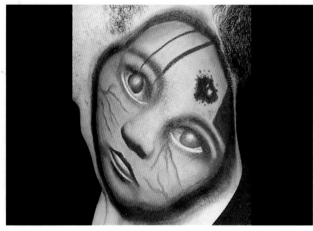

Brandon is well known for his use of blue.

thing other than simply saying hello to everyone involved…that is without doing a single tattoo."

He now counts himself as the CEO of at least four enterprises. His street shop All or Nothing has expanded to include A.N.T.I. Art Elite, a luxurious, high-end shop for appointment-only, large-scale work clients. This spa-like environment boasts two movie theaters with thousands of titles, two indoor koi ponds, and two art galleries housing Brandon's private collection of paintings and other fine art from some the world's best tattooists. The studio is also stocked with wireless video games in every room, a hot tub, hand-laid Brazilian flooring, sandblasted and etched glass, and a grill stocked with gourmet-quality refreshments. Clients who fly in to get tattooed by Brandon or one of the other artists on his team are treated with pick-up and drop-off service, and Brandon's staff typically arranges all of these clients' accommodations in the manner of a high-end concierge service.

In addition to the two tattoo studios, Brandon manages Stranglehold Merchandise, which is largely an e-commerce venture. Through the website StrangleholdMerch.com, Brandon sells accessories, tattoo aftercare products, art, tattoo equipment and machines, clothing (both for humans and dogs), stickers, DVDs, and even weapons. Stranglehold Merchandise is the landing page for many of Brandon's promotional projects, and he has made a tidy business of selling his wares to the adoring public.

His fourth business is the All or Nothing Pit Bull Rescue, which is dedicated to rescuing fighting pit bulls, rehabilitating them, and matching them with loving homes. His own family dogs, two beautiful pits named Cain and Medusa, were abused as fighting dogs before Brandon and his wife helped to rehabilitate them. His experience with the breed inspired him to take advantage of his success as a businessman, and to give back through the development of the rescue.

Some of the first dogs he was able to help were rescued from disgraced football star Michael Vick. After three of Vick's abused dogs landed at the Georgia SPCA, Brandon took two of them to the All Or Nothing Pit Bull Rescue, where they have undergone a great deal of rehabilitation and socialization.

One of Brandon's most impressive accomplishments as a businessman is his knack for self-promotion. While his acclaim in the industry is well deserved—as his unique, vibrant art speaks for his talent—many talented artists in the tattoo world do not reach Brandon's level of notoriety. He has harnessed the power of the Internet, the tattoo media, and the growing popularity of tattoo art to brand himself.

As the world of tattooing has long been somewhat closed off from mainstream society, some in the industry resent Brandon's machine-like self-promotion. He responds in Whore, "I am selling myself, reaching further out…investing, saving, scraping, piling profits. All these obscure, lazy, drunken tattoo artists who impress each other with their anonymity and despise me for my oversaturated, overrated levels of exposure will continue to starve long after I'm done tattooing."

His response to the criticism may be harsh, but Brandon makes a valid point. He expects to be done building his empire soon, and he looks forward to a long retirement in an industry that isn't known for such success.

In addition to serving as the chief executive for his four businesses, Brandon maintains a 40-plus-hour per week schedule of tattooing. He explains that, although he loves his life, his tendency to become consumed by his business has cost him heavily:

"I love tattooing, and I have given everything I have to tattooing," he says. "It has saved my life, but at the same time it has destroyed my life. Running four businesses is really four full-time jobs, and I still tattoo a full schedule. The cost has been immense—my family life, my marriage, my sanity, my friendships all have suffered for the greater good of my career. I am spread way too thin, and am desperately trying to find some kind of balance. I have not found it yet, if anything it's getting worse. The hours I am working are ridiculous."

HIS BACKGROUND

Brandon was raised on an isolated island off the coast of Florida called Perdido Key. While the area has been developed somewhat in recent years, Brandon recalls a time when the beach was empty.

"I grew up on the beach back when no one was around—no condos, no people...not much of any-

Here is the underside of Brandon's "Devil's Rejects" sleeve.

Vivid colors highlight this jungle sleeve.

An uncommon combination of blues and reds creates an intriguing contrast.

The color saturation in this Halloween chest piece is intense.

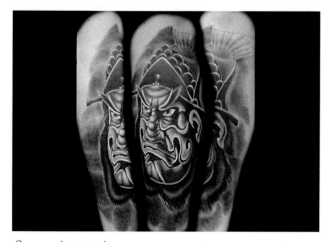

Samurai portrait

thing. I became very good at entertaining myself and living in solitude," he explains. "There were no kids on the island except my family. I created art all the time. It was a way to keep myself busy and entertained. It was an amazing situation to grow up in, and it taught me a lot. Both of my parents are incredible and supportive, so I was blessed for sure."

He credits his parents, and his father in particular, with giving him the work ethic that has helped him to build his business so rapidly and to achieve such great heights in his art. In Whore, he explains that his father "worked from the time he was five years old, every day. He came from absolute poverty and starvation to become an unstoppable force of financial domination. He retired before I completed high school, finally finding contentment. As the dust from his workaholism settled, he became a different person."

His father's influence and success shaped Brandon's own plans for himself, and he always names his father as the one who taught him the importance of persistence in achieving his life's goals.

IN HIS OWN WORDS: BRANDON BOND Q&A

Q: Where did you get your start tattooing?

A: I did a formal apprenticeship under Jim Wolfe at Tattoo Zoo in Fort Walton Beach, Florida.

Q: How long have you been tattooing?

A: It's a blur—something like 16 years or so now. I'm bad at math. That's why I had to become an artist!

Q: What made you decide to become a tattoo artist?

A: I was not making enough money to survive being a musician.

Q: Who were some of the artists you admired when you got started on your tattoo career?

A: Bob Tyrell, Paul Booth, Jim Wolfe, Albie Rock, Chris Trevino, and Damon Conklin

Q: Whom do you admire now?

A: Dave Tedder, Sean Herman, Chris Vennekamp, Tim Orth, Jace Masula, Short, John Lloyd, Matt Dunlap…Really, everyone who has ever worked at All or Nothing tattoos here in Atlanta.

Q: You frequently mention your father as an

inspiration to your work ethic, but what else has been a significant influence? What shapes the decisions you've made as an artist?

A: At this point in my career, all of my decisions seem to be based on my schedule. I am a slave to my appointment book.

Q: And speaking of your schedule, you are known for being as good as a marketer for your business as you are an artist. Tell me about your most recent promotional efforts.

A: We promote our work as hard as we can at All or Nothing—television, films, DVDs, websites, mailing lists, YouTube…really a zillion ways. It has changed through the years because the outlets for promotion have changed. When I started tattooing, there was no Internet. Now there are all the social networks—MySpace, Facebook, InkedNation…We have adjusted our approach to keep up with the times, for sure.

Q: Where do your business efforts intersect with your creative work?

A: It's fluid and frustrating for sure. I am an artist first, yes, but if you looked in my schedule book, you might wonder how I keep my focus. It is an uncomfortable intersection for many people and for many tattoo crews. I think what has made us so successful at All or Nothing is in part simply finding a way to accomplish both good business and customer service while keeping an extremely high level of art consistently.

Q: Does one get in the way of the other? Do you ever think that the business side of your work overshadows the artistic side, or vice-versa?

A: Yes. Every single waking moment, the two are opposing forces in my life. It's driving me nuts! It's the most frustrating aspect of my day-to-day life. I hate being a businessman and dealing with the suits and accountants and lawyers and real estate weirdoes and advertisers. It sucks.

On the creative side, it's an evolutionary journey. All art is an evolution, or it becomes stagnant. I have been through both experiences—change and stagnancy—many times in my life and in my career. At times, it comes like fire, and at other times, there are just too many distractions.

Q: Do you have much time for a social life?

A: What's a social life? I used to have friends and go to football games and party and stuff, but

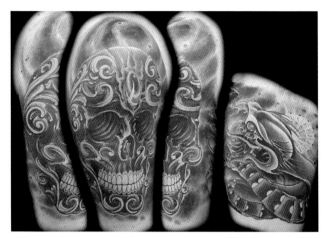

Notice the depth of the eye sockets in this skull with snake.

Brandon's signature piece—his take on Darth Vader is perhaps his best-known tattoo.

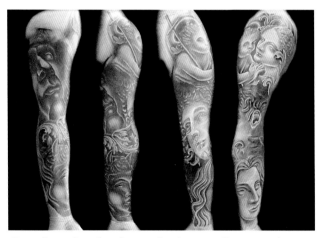

Brandon often heightens the drama of a tattoo by zooming in on faces instead of presenting whole figures.

This sleeve is based on images from Brandon Bond's favorite film, "The Devil's Rejects."

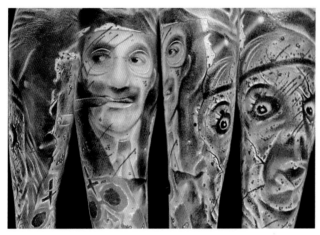

This sleeve is also based on images from Brandon Bond's favorite film, "The Devil's Rejects."

Brandon created this beautiful lion portrait with very few hard lines, giving it a soft, watercolor effect.

recently, there has been none of that. I am grateful for all the success, but the demands on my time and my patience are outgrowing my ability to keep up at this point. I've been going hard for way too long. It's time for a change in my life for sure. We are working toward that now.

Q: When you're not tattooing, what do you like to do?

A: You're asking me this question when I haven't had a day off in two months, so honestly now is a pretty rough time to answer it. I do like to spend time with my dogs, and I like to wreck my golf cart. Other than that, I'm always working on something.

Q: How did you end up in Atlanta?

A: The airport in Atlanta is one of the biggest in the country, and the gun laws in the state of Georgia are superb! Hah!

The truth is, I knew that we would end up having a lot of out-of-state and international clientele when I opened these shops, and the convenience of Atlanta's airport allows us to offer airport shuttle services, hotel and food arrangements…the whole shebang! It's easy for anybody to get a direct flight to Atlanta pretty easily and affordably, and it's an easy city to get around.

I love Atlanta…the changing seasons and the southern vibe, the music and the big rims…all the sports teams…and the people in Atlanta are awesome!

Q: What's your impression of the tattoo scene in Atlanta? It's a city with several well-known shops.

A: Atlanta has an extremely large and extremely diverse tattoo community. There are a lot of incredible shops here, and like everywhere, a lot of not-so-incredible ones as well. My guys at All or Nothing are kept pretty busy with reworks and cover-ups for sure!

There is such a huge community here, and it's amazing. I'm glad to be a part of it, and I'm glad to have been able to add to it. I'm friends with many other shop owners, and others don't seem to want to be friends. It's kind of weird.

Q: Do you have a favorite tattoo out of your portfolio?

A: Yes! I like the "Devil's Rejects" sleeve (top two images) I did, mostly because it's based on images that we stole from my favorite movie. Also, the client let me do whatever I wanted on him. I love that experience. It always makes for the best tattoo work. Artistic freedom is really where it's at.

Q: Do you see yourself changing as an artist? Have you noticed any new trends?

A: Yes, every day! Art is a fluid journey, or it is a stagnant experience. The flow of new, young, and amazing artists at All or Nothing keeps me on my toes! These kids are amazing. I do my best just to keep up with my staff.

My newer works are unlike anything I have ever done before, and they're not like anything I think I've seen anyone else do, either. No one has seen pictures of the newest sleeves and stuff because they aren't complete yet. I'm really into the latest stuff that I've been working on. It is an entirely different approach.

Q: What do you think makes your work stand out? How could we pick one of your tattoos out of a lineup?

A: It took a long time and a lot of work for people to be able to recognize my work simply by glancing at it, but I do believe my work is recognizable now, both color work and black and gray.

Art is subjective, so it's kind of a hard question to answer. However, I have seen the style of artwork that we were doing at All or Nothing when we opened grow into a huge amount of common art. I believe our styles and the styles we've developed together have had a profound impact on the tattoo industry. Pick up any tattoo magazine, and you will see what I'm talking about. It's awesome.

I'm not bitching about it at all...some artists don't like it when others bite off their styles. I think it's pretty cool.

Q: Do you identify with a particular style of tattooing?

A: Well, I believe that, at All or Nothing, we have had a large influence on contemporary styles, so I feel like my work falls in line with the cutting edge. The cutting edge is based on our style. But seriously, I am really excited about all the new art that's coming out. There is a renaissance happening now in tattooing, and I'm glad to be a part of it.

Q: What do you think of the industry today, and this renaissance in particular?

A: I think it's growing faster than anyone is willing to admit. I have seen nothing but growth

While Brandon is best known for color, he is also a master of black and gray.

These hand tattoos bear Brandon's trademark blues.

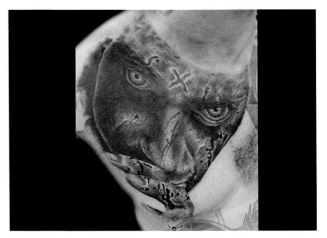

The placement of this tattoo highlights the natural musculature of the wearer's chest.

for the two decades I've been a part of it, with no end in sight. I think the changes in the industry have been too vast and numerous to list, honestly. Artists are changing, clients are changing, shops are changing, promotions are changing, communication is changing…everything about what we thought we knew is changing. It's incredible, and it's extremely exciting. New technologies, young artists, new inks, new tattoo machines, new levels of art and saturation…every day brings something different for us to adapt to and grow towards. It's the bees' knees!

Q: Have there been times in your career when you felt like you reached a stopping place?

A: Yes. When I was touring way too much and running both the shops at the same time and tattooing full-time and All or Nothing was growing so fast. Tattooing took a back seat, and it had to be put on hold for a while. However, I believe that the crew that works here with me helps me through that, and collaborative tattooing always helps when I'm feeling overworked or like I've reached a creative plateau. The act of two artists working together on a piece always strengthens both artists. We do a lot of two-artists-on-one-client tattooing here.

Q: You've slowed down quite a bit in your touring schedule. How did traveling so much earlier in your career impact your life?

A: I toured nonstop for over a decade. Some years, I did more than 30 shows in only 52 weeks, which meant being out of town more [often] than every other week. One week home…then two, three, even four weeks on the road. It was crazy—airports, hotels, rental cars, room service, guest appearances and guest spots, long hours, delayed flights, crazy women, partying, and debauchery. It was an amazing time in my life, and it was something I'll never forget or regret. It got my name out there more than anything else I could have done.

That part of my life is over now. My crew of amazingly talented tattoo artists from All or Nothing do the touring nowadays. They deserve the attention, and my presence is simply a distraction to what they are doing.

I stopped touring two years ago, and I will probably never do a tattoo anywhere on the road ever again. I had my fill of the madness, and I enjoyed every second of it. My guys still attend at least 25 shows a year, which means that every other week a couple of my guys are on the road to somewhere, tattooing at all hours of the day and night. More power to 'em! They are doing a great job winning awards and doing great art without me. I'm learning from them now.

This full-coverage chest piece embodies a variety of themes.

Here is Brandon's lifelike take on James Dean.

But even the "eternal rebel" has fallen under the spell of Brandon's blues.

Angel in a blue gown stands out against a fiery background.

Judicious use of color adds highlight to this girl with skull.

Sharp lines and muted colors are combined to produce the ethereal quality of this child's face.

Girl with dead baby offers a great way to showcase Brandon's blues!

Chapter Two

Sunny Buick

Expatriate Artiste

What's inside a girl? Sugar, spice, and everything nice, of course. On the outside, she's a candy-coated illusion of sweetness. Inwardly, she's famished for all that's out of reach, forced a diet of self-loathing in search for perfection, a sweet confection feeding on herself, recycling her identity from what she culls from the outside. Corrosive like sugar to the teeth. She seeks her sanctuary inwardly and cannibalizes it. Hungry because she shouldn't take too much. Taking too much because she's so hungry.
—Sunny Buick, "Manifesto"

Sunny works out many of her thoughts on gender and spirituality through such paintings as her "Vision in a Bathtub."

Sunny Buick got her start in the tattoo industry 16 years ago, and she has taken a long, complicated trip to become the artist she is today. She is widely respected both for her unique take on traditional American tattooing, and for her incorporation of tattoo-style elements into her fine art. She has lived and worked all over the world, seen her tattoos published in many international magazines, had her art featured in gallery exhibitions, and even written articles and organized her own gallery showings. She is well known in the lowbrow art world as well as among tattooists, particularly those practicing the Traditional American style that Sunny has embraced.

Tattooists are unique in the art world in that they are not creating their images in a vacuum. When asked about the inspiration behind their art, many tattooists will say that it's not really about them, their style, or their message. Tattoo artists frequently think of themselves as providing a service to a client; thus the client's philosophies and desires for

Sunny also found inspiration in the Chinese neighborhoods as she grew up in San Francisco.

Sunny spent a lot of time in the Mexican neighborhoods of San Francisco, and the influence is apparent in the Day of the Dead skulls she frequently incorporates in her tattoos.

19

Painting by Sunny Buick

the final outcome often supercede the artist's own. While the best artists certainly have a definable style, they are most often as concerned with pleasing the client as they are with translating their personal philosophies or creative messages into a tattooed image.

Sunny Buck, however, takes a slightly different approach. In the tradition of the 20th century avant-garde, she takes her own creative philosophy so seriously that she has created a manifesto of her artistic intentions. Combining ideas culled from feminism, fine art, carnival life, and her own creative instinct, Sunny has developed a signature style in her tattoos as well as her paintings.

HER BACKGROUND

Born in British Columbia to a single, hippie mother, Sunny moved around quite a bit as a child, but she spent much of her time in California. Around the age of 15, she landed in San Francisco.

She explains, "I was greatly influenced by this town. The Mexican and Chinese neighborhoods totally had an effect on the colorful imagery that I produce." These cultures are echoed in the bold reds, yellows, pinks and greens that permeate both Sunny's tattoo and fine art. She also has borrowed thematic elements from them.

For instance, a frequent theme borrowed from the Mexican culture (page 19) Sunny encountered during her time in San Francisco includes the Sugar Skull, which she recreates with a traditional American tattoo flavor. In her "Manifesto," she explains her attraction to this imagery, "I think the

Sunny uses bold lines and bright, primary colors in the style of Traditional American tattooing.

skull is part of our inner beauty. It's what's inside us; our personalities are housed mostly in our heads. [It's] the image of mortality that we leave behind when we die, and hopefully our art will endure with it. Animated bones to me are the most joyous image, as if death were just a big joke."

Sunny had always been creative, and she knew as a young woman that she hoped to pursue art as a career. She decided to become a tattoo artist because she thought she could make a living from her own art instead of "what some art director wanted from me. Plus," she explains, "I was really attracted to the history and mystery of tattooing. I think I also wanted a career where I could be my own little freaky self and not have to conform. I'm also not very good at getting up in the morn-

In Sunny's spider lady half-sleeve, the disturbing truth is not far beneath the surface.

The iconography of this deceptively simple "Lily" reveals Sunny's depth as a painter.

ing, and tattooing is good for night owls."

She is also drawn to the world of carnival freaks. Her own grandmother was born without arms, and Sunny identified with the sideshow world and became interested in exploring this outsider's reality more intensively. She says, "You may notice my obsession with freaks…I'm fascinated by what it must be like to be a Siamese twin, to be chained for life to the same person, who also shares your moment-to-moment existence, all the way down to your DNA…I sometimes feel that there's a Siamese twin inside us all, a part of us that maybe we'd like to abandon, but we can't."

Tattooing has a long association with the carnival and other folks who tend to linger

21

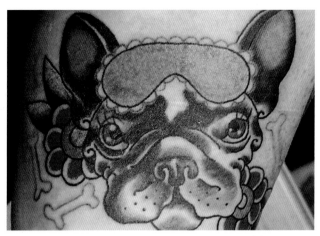

This sweet puppy is rendered in unmistakable Sunny Buick style.

The Traditional American influence is apparent here.

The details in the black linework make this piece uniquely Sunny Buick's.

along the fringes of society, so it gave her an opportunity to explore these themes as her career progressed.

She began exploring her options to find an apprenticeship, and struggled for several years to find the right place to learn. As many artists do, she started out "the wrong way," working with a friend who tattooed at his house, then continuing in her own home once she'd learned some of the basics. After four years of searching for an apprenticeship, she landed one with Henry Goldfield of Goldfield's Tattoo Studio.

Goldfield's Tattoo was established in San Francisco in 1977, and Henry had developed a reputation for being one of the pioneers of modern tattooing in the city. Apprenticeship under Henry was rigorous, as he was one of the few artists in the area offering the traditional seven-year apprentice program at the time. Sunny explains, "His shop and style corresponded with me perfectly. I had to ask him twice for an apprenticeship before it matched up, but it was great when it did. No one at the time ever had made it through his full seven-year program. In the end, neither did I. I got fired after six years."

From her meticulous training, however, Sunny mastered the basics of tattooing, as is evident in her precise color work, her classic straight-black traditional shading, and her crisp, clean lines. When she was turned loose from Goldfield's, she was ready to go out on her own.

HER STYLE

Sunny's style is distinctly Traditional American. From the bold outlines to the straight black shading, from the themes of beautiful women, skulls, and guns…her work reflects her inheritance from classic American tattooing, both in terms of style and content. As with many traditional-style tattooists, one of the attractions for Sunny is that it will look good for many years. All tattoos will fade with time, but the traditional American approach is known for retaining its integrity better than many other approaches. "I leave a lot of open skin," she explains. "I'm more concerned with the tattoo looking good in 50 years than blowing people away with super realism or over coloring."

In her classic pairing of barn swallows—(page 20) which is a common traditional American theme—on a woman's feet, the images are rendered through clean lines and solid coloring. Her emphasis is not on creating any illusion of realism; the birds are stylized and two-dimensional. She leaves negative space in the tattoo instead of saturating the skin with color in the style of many modern-day tattooists, and the only shading in the wings is achieved through straight black ink instead of variations in color or the use of a range of grays. The effect is a simple, clean image that will likely appear just as bold in several decades as it does while brand new.

Sunny makes the style unique, however, by including distinctly feminine touches, such as the delicate blue line work in the banners, the sweet little hearts and stars, and the flowing script. Traditional American work is often very bold and masculine, but Sunny softens it by including

these unique details. "I don't think I'm doing anything overly original," she expounds, "Just traditional stuff with my own touch."

What is truly unique about Sunny's style, however, is her juxtaposition of the sweet and the creepy to create a sort of visual dissonance in the viewer's mind. Her tattoos appear to be

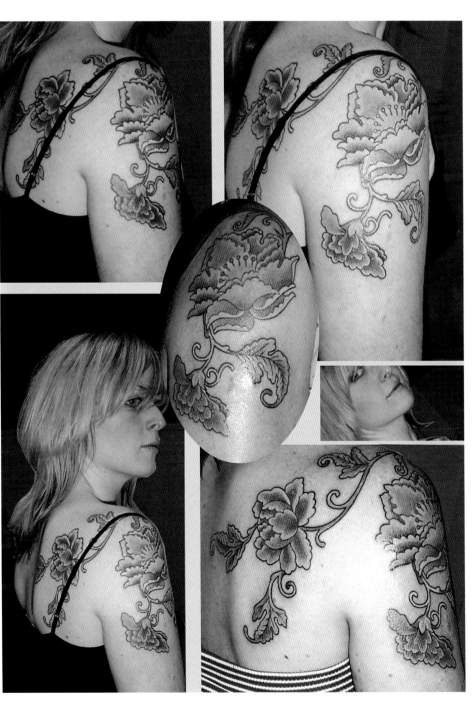

Sunny puts negative space to superb use in this floral work.

  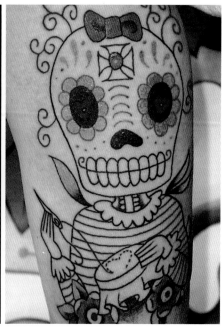

The Mexican Day of the Dead meets Traditional American styling.

Sunny has spent much of her career in Paris, and her work shows it in ways both obvious and subtle.

Leave it to Sunny to come up with a unique take on the sugar skull theme.

bright, feminine, and naive, but there is always something sinister lurking just beneath the surface. She explains this tension in her manifesto, "I am still that only child who found a little reassurance in a world of her own fantasies, but somewhere deeper, there's my feminine intuition."

Take a look at her spider lady half-sleeve (page 21), for instance. On the surface, there is a somewhat silly image. The female face is idealized, with impossibly green eyes and hyper-stylized blond hair, carefully rendered in perfect ringlets. Her tiny, red lips and cute nose are perfect examples of our romanticized image of female beauty. The spider legs that creepily surround this face are rendered in cartoon fashion, masking to a certain degree the horrid creature Sunny has created. The disturbing truth, however, is not buried far beneath the surface in this piece.

Sunny also suggests that much of this tension between surface-level beauty and the darkness lying underneath stems from her gender. In her "Manifesto," she describes this tension, "I think I know a little about beauty; a

great deal of my life has been spent pondering its mystery…devouring fashion magazines, sentenced to perpetual diets, reaching for an impossible ideal that has marked me since birth." Many of the characters that she features in her tattoos and in her fine art are female, and she says, "I've faithfully studied the feminine mystique and how to conjure an illusion to pacify this ruthless ideal that has haunted women through the ages." In Sunny's vision, the feminine mystique is a suspension between opposing forces: purity and filth, spirituality and materialism, beauty and terror. She describes it as being, "Trapped between narcissism and dependency, a target of consumerism…Girls are forever in a state of suspension. How desperate, then, the quest for this girlish imagery to resolve the trauma, finding therapeutic feelings of safety in something hauntingly familiar."

HER PAINTINGS

Nowhere is this suspension between various polarities more apparent than in Sunny's paintings. For instance, in her "Vision in a Bathtub" painting (page 18), she uses another highly idealized, blond figure to illustrate the division between spirituality and materialism. The woman has the familiar rosy cheeks, stylized hair, and ideal proportions of the female figures in traditional American tattoo art. Her pink skin, blue eyes, and impossibly buoyant breasts mark her as a beautiful woman—nearly a fetish figure in our society. Above her head, Sunny has created a pantheon of world religion, inviting the figure to explore her spirituality. Beneath her, there are candles, jewels, soaps, perfumes, and all the material attractions that we associate with the mask of femininity. Sunny enhances the symbolism by placing the figure in a bathtub. Symbolically, she is becoming cleaner, more pure, and perhaps readying herself for the spiritual experience that awaits; on the other hand, she is in a bathtub that is clearly filled with perfumes, soaps, and other products…she is submerged in a world of illusion and materialism.

Here's another sugar skull, this one with a gambling theme.

Similarly, in her "Lily" painting (page 21), Sunny simultaneously portrays many of the traditional ideas and myths of femininity. The face of the creature is cute, with large, innocent eyes; however, it has the body of a snake. The association in Christian art between Eve and the serpent emerges, but the soft, baby-pink background and the cartoon-like face of the creature creates a tension in the viewer. The image of a glass jar also recalls the Christian association of the Virgin Mary as a chalice or Holy Grail. In this deceptively simple piece, Sunny makes a statement on femininity and Christian iconography.

SUNNY TODAY

Sunny currently lives in Paris, France, and she travels frequently to work. She works

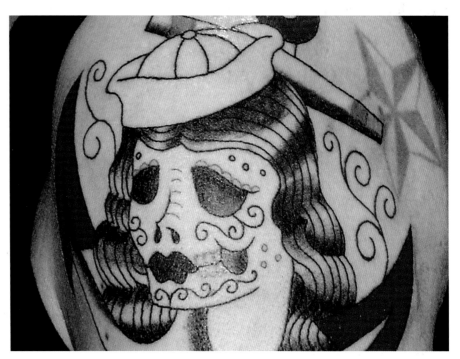

Sunny frequently plays with tattoo's historical connection to sailing.

25

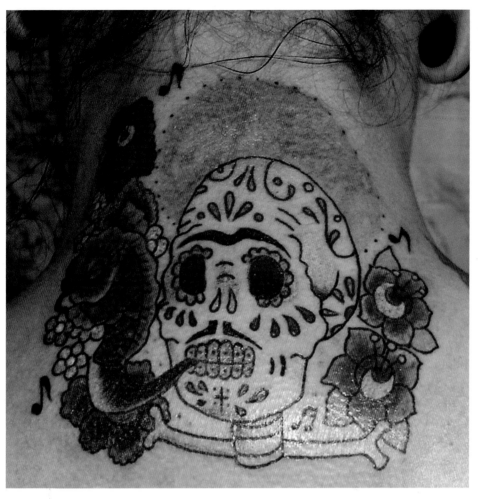

Sunny cites the Surrealists as some of her strongest influences.

is working to generate interest in her work. She explains, "I finally reached the point here where I'm doing only my style of custom tattoos. I don't hang around with other tattooers here, but I have a few tattooer friends scattered all over Europe. In France, a new style is being developed that uses a lot of black, is very abstract, and is sometimes purposely hyper-naïve."

While life on the road is inevitably exhausting, Sunny is happy with her life and work. As the tattoo industry changes, she has changed along with it, and she expects to continue to grow with the industry she has embraced: "It's a great time to make a living in this industry. I guess it's kinda missing the old romance and magic of the circus sideshow days…but I don't know. I didn't live back then. I'm happy with my lifestyle!"

one week each month in a private studio in Paris, and she splits the rest of her time between shops in Lyon, France; Milan, Italy; and Berlin, Germany. She explains her decision to make Paris her home base; "I always wanted to speak French, and I had the idea to live here to become fluent."

She describes the tattoo scene in Paris as unique, with its own set of stereotypes that are quite different from the way we generally think of tattooed people. "The French aren't as tattooed as the Italians and the English," she says. "Still, the French are very conscious of fashion, and I'm quite exotic to them."

While her style is unique in tattooing anywhere, it goes particularly against the grain in Paris. But because she's a bit of a maverick, it

Sunny Buick was born in Canada, raised in California, and now lives and works in Paris, France.

26

In Her Own Words: Sunny Buick Q & A

Q: You travel a lot as a part of the way you've set up your work schedule. Do you make it to many shows?

A: I do. Conventions are stressful, but they are also inspiring. Doing shows is the most effective way of getting a "name" in the business. However, doing shows is very hard on the body. I like the Milan convention because the Italians are really warm and expressive.

Q: What else do you do to promote your work?

A: I use the P.T. Barnum method of promotion…I harass the press! I also participate in a lot of art shows and tattoo conventions, and that helps to get my name out there. It's

Another combination of themes results in this butterfly lady.

This carousel horse has a Traditional flair.

This sugar skull is embellished with a dagger.

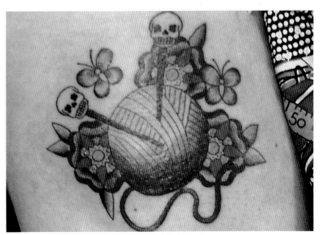

The theme here appears to be, "knit or die!"

27

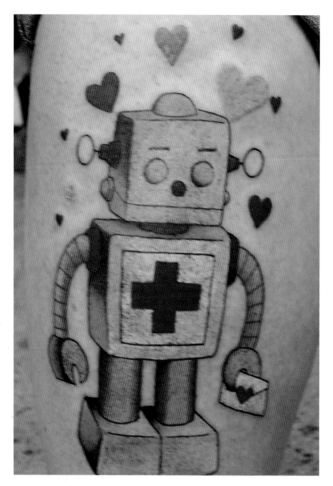

Sunny applies her distinctive, feminine touch to a cold subject to achieve some interesting effects.

changed through the years with the Internet. There are sites like MySpace, Etsy, and blogs that I use now. I also sometimes send something to magazines that I like.

Q: With all the traveling that you do, do you have much of a time for a private life?

A: I do. I like sewing, reading, watching movies, cooking, and listening to music when I'm not tattooing.

Tattooing is often difficult on family life, though, because we are married first to our jobs. A lot of spouses are jealous of our love for our work or don't understand how hard it is. They just think we have fun all day. I'm often away from home, and sometimes I'm only home one week per month. It's hard on my husband.

Luckily, he has his passions as well that occupy him, and he's not jealous. He's just happy that I do what I love!

Q: For you, what's the business side of being an artist like?

A: I never opened my own shop because I'm afraid of the responsibility of the business side of tattooing. Plus, I don't think I have the energy anymore. I'd rather enjoy my life and live a little more on the cheap, beatnik style. I'm afraid I'll regret it when I want to retire for good.

Q: Are there any really memorable clients you've had through the years?

A: The best story is a tattoo I never got a chance to do. A transsexual artist once solicited me to tattoo a wood grain pattern on the scars of her shattered leg as an ironic tribute to her "almost" lost part. She would have had a wooden leg.

This beautiful pin-up is done in the classic Traditional American style.

This Traditional style nurse portrait will stand the test of time.

A sugar skull goes well with a music theme.

This Lucky Cat reflects some of Sunny's Asian influence, but it's rendered in the Traditional style.

Painting by Sunny Buick

She had been involved in an accident with a car while on her bike. She also did a monthly illustration in a very high profile car magazine, but she was part of the anti-car bicycle movement in San Francisco. I think the accident reinforced her hatred of cars.

She brought me an image from Magritte, and God knows I love the surrealists. I regret I didn't get to do it because symbolically, I thought it was fantastic! My artistic vocabulary can't help but be affected by this kind of influence…the regenerative aspects of tattooing, the lifestyle, the stories, the transformation of skin and body…the ultimate canvas!

Painting by Sunny Buick

Q: Do you have a favorite piece that you've done? If so, what is it?

A: I have a number of favorite pieces, but it always seems to be the last one that I was quite satisfied with that's my favorite. I'm quite fond of some crafty themed tattoos I've done because I guess they reflect some things I'm involved with recently.

Q: Do you think you're still changing as an artist?

A: I feel freer to put myself into the designs. People are coming to me, to Sunny Buick, to get a tattoo done in my style, not just passing by a shop to get something done by anybody.

Painting by Sunny Buick

Sunny often combines traditional American tattoo elements with the Mexican and Asian influences.

Q: *Have there been times when you felt like you were reaching a plateau as an artist?*

A: Sometimes, I get burned out on tattooing, and I've always painted to get through it. I purposely try to paint "tattoo fantasies," like covering a painted girl's body in tattoos like a sideshow personality, just to get re-inspired. I always end up missing the contact with my customers, so after a phase of feeling burned out, I get jazzed up and come back to work.

Q: *Who were some of the artists that you admired early in your career? And who do you think is influential now?*

A: I used to admire Ed Hardy, Jill Jordan, and Sailor Jerry. Nowadays, I admire so many Italian tattoo artists! Really, there's so much incredible stuff being done in Italy. What am I doing in France?

Q: *What influences have helped shape the career you've established for yourself?*

A: I guess everything I see and experience influences me. My personality and destiny have shaped my decisions more than anything. Decisions are hard, and sometimes it's best to wait to have all the elements you are sure about in place. Then, the right decision is clearer. This is true at least in painting and tattooing when I'm not sure about what colors to use.

Q: *What do you remember about the first tattoo you ever did?*

A: I remember thinking, "This isn't so hard at all!" Later, it became harder. And it seems to get harder physically and mentally with each year that passes. What's that about?

Painting by Sunny Buick

Q: *Do you think you've gone through many phases as an artist?*

A: I think I've pretty much remained true to my own style. I really haven't changed very much, just gotten a little more polished. I've seen colleagues go through drastic style changes. Maybe they were still searching for themselves…

Painting by Sunny Buick

Chapter Three

Dan Henk

The Art of Horror

"I spend up to 80 hours a week making art—tattooing and drawing. I wouldn't do anything else," says Dan Henk. "If I won the lottery tomorrow, I'd still do art."

Like many tattooists, Dan lives and breathes his trade. It's more than just a living for him; it's a way of life. He is constantly on the move between the shops where he works, and he spends the time that he isn't tattooing working on various other projects. Much of his art is dark and

Dan Henk draws inspiration from a lifetime of dark experiences.

inspired by the horror genre; however, his zeal for his creative endeavors comes from a much brighter place.

HIS BACKGROUND

Dan grew up as a bona fide Army brat, so he can't quite say where he's from. "I've lived in Kentucky, Tennessee, Germany, Florida, North Carolina, Virginia, Washington, DC, upstate New York, and now near New York City," he explains. "Everywhere you've been molds you or influences you in some way, but I can't say that anywhere has ever been my home. The constant moving, though, does encourage an outsider status. Kids are cruel, and you always end up being the new kid on the block when you move to a new place."

Perhaps because of these experiences, Dan became interested in punk rock as a teenager, and he credits it for reinforcing this outsider's perspective. He says, "It really was pivotal in the way I think. I do my own thing, and if you don't like it, that's not my problem. People are way too concerned about other people."

This attitude put Dan at odds with his family, which he describes as "super religious, plus, my Dad is an Army Colonel." He ran away from home repeatedly as a kid, and his family kicked him out at the age of 18. He spent eight months homeless, "Like, living in the woods homeless. It was never good."

After drifting for a few years, Dan decided to go to art school at the age of 23. There he learned quite a bit about being a professional artist, then he decided to drop out early to go to work. He began getting gigs as an illustrator for album covers, band art, and published a few of his paintings in art books. While he

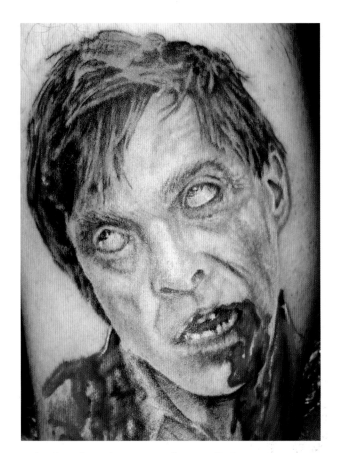

The details and textures of Dan's fly boy tattoo give an impressive illusion of reality.

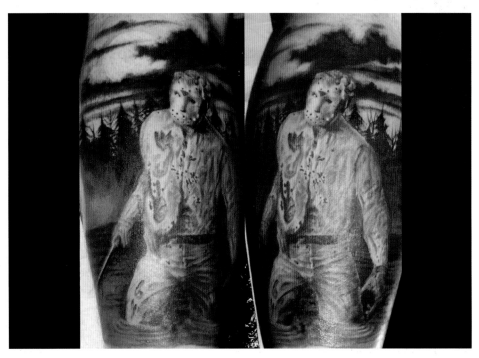

Here is Dan's interpretation of Jason Voorhees from "Friday the 13th."

This painting features Dan's deceased wife Monica.

American-style tattooing. "That style is fine, and if well-done, I definitely respect it. I even have some of it on me. That's not what I wanted to do for a living, though.

"I went to art school, and I'd interviewed with some comic and book companies. That style was the avenue I wanted to pursue. I enjoy realistic images, and I realized that tattooing would allow me to create realistically and give me the freedom to pick and choose my own work." Dan still takes side-jobs for books, magazines, art galleries, and bands, but he has embraced the creative freedom that tattooing offered him.

After Dan had been tattooing for about a year, he recalls an article in *Tattoo Planet Magazine* featuring Guy Aitchison again, and he remembers this moment as providing him even more enthusiasm for his new career. "He was so

Dan's wife Monica was killed by an unidentified hit-and-run driver.

enjoyed the notoriety, he struggled to make ends meet with the irregular work of a freelance artist. Then, Dan's brother connected him with Chad Divel of Ink Addiction in Carlisle, Pennsylvania. Chad was looking for an apprentice, and he had been impressed with Dan's skill as a painter and illustrator. He offered him the position. Dan remembers, "I saved up $2,000, bought two Time Machines and a set of Starbright inks, and it's been a rocky road ever since!"

Dan did not recognize the possibility of tattooing as a career for many years because he'd never been exposed to the artistic potential that was developing in tattoo art at the time; but when he stumbled on some images of work by Guy Aitchison, he became inspired by the possibilities. "I realized it was more than just old school," he explains, referring to Traditional

good, and the work so effortlessly followed the flow of the skin," he says. "It really opened my eyes."

His Style

In the eight intervening years, Dan has developed a name for himself in the tattoo industry as the go-to guy for highly realistic horror work. Both in his fine art and in his tattooing, the images are often collected from our dark side, either from Dan's own imagination or in society's collective imagination as it emerges in our cinema.

From fine details in the hair and eyes of the creatures he tattoos, we see the influence of Dan's interest in illustration and comics. In his fly boy tattoo, for instance (page 35), the creases in the face, the details in the hair's texture, and the seeming sheen on the blood that drips from the mouth all give an impressive illusion of reality. Similarly, in his interpretation of horror icon Jason Voorhees, he recreates much of the realism that made the movie famous in the tattoo. The texture of the clothing, including that which is meant to appear wet, the surface details of the water, and the background forest all emerge from the skin with fantastic realism. Dan suspends the disbelief of the viewer, inviting us to accept the unlikely figures. He is humble about his approach, suggesting, "I'm influenced by other artists, but they are a piece in the grand scheme of things. I try to incorporate what I like from others, but not to copy them outright. I think my stuff tends to be a little more textured and detailed, a little more dark and creepy than most. Maybe I'm just fooling myself, but that's what I shoot for."

Dan describes his own

Impressive realism runs throughout Dan's take on Jack Nicholson's character from "The Shining." Notice the translucent glow that Dan achieves with simple black and gray tones.

Dan's uniquely dark perspective sets the mood of his workspace, matching the tattoos he applies.

Notice the details and textures that Dan captures with black and grey tones.

Dan's "Reanimator" has a haunting glow, both in the flesh and in the syringe.

This tattoo of a fetal skeleton in a liquor jar is one of Dan's favorites.

burgeoning awareness of his style of art as emerging in art school. He explains, "I didn't think I really had a style when I first started art school. I just rendered things the way I saw them.

Painting by Dan Henk

Everyone kept talking about my distinct style, but I didn't see it. I just painted and drew the way I saw the world." He came to recognize that his outlook was unique, however, through the years of working as an artist. "I grew to understand how my view of the world was different," he explains. "Love it or hate it, I have a unique perspective. I don't try to focus on what might be new or different or appealing. Regardless, that never works, even if you do make it your focus. I just try to do projects I'm into, and I render them as I envision them."

Perhaps Dan's sinister vision of realism comes

from his own difficult experiences. From his own bout of homelessness to recent events in his personal life, Dan's complicated existence has given him many opportunities to come face to face with death.

While he was homeless, he says, "I was stabbed by a crackhead in Washington, D.C. I had to have the tendon of my left thumb reattached from that experience. Later, I was in a car accident and my head went through the windshield. A few years later, in 2001, I came down with brain cancer, and I was in the Intensive Care Unit in Bellevue when the Twin Towers went down. Six years later, my wife was killed by a hit and run driver, and no one was ever caught. Not to cry poor me, but what you go through in life makes you what you are." Dan has seen his share of the dark side, and the dark expressions in his

Painting by Dan Henk

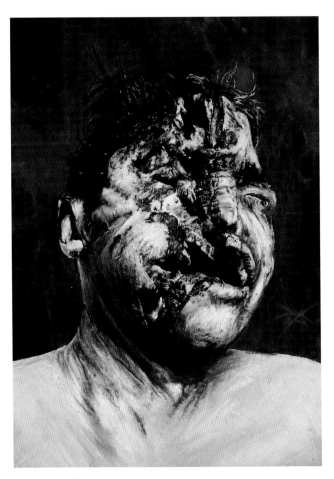

Painting by Dan Henk

paintings and tattoos reflect these experiences.

Even down to the details of what he includes in his own workspace (page 37), Dan's uniquely dark perspective shines true. From various skulls to creepy art, he sets his working scene with a mood that matches the tattoos he applies there.

Dan also likes to credit the artists whom he respects as being influential in the development of his own style. He credits Robert Hernandez for inspiring him to view the overlap between illustration and tattooing: "Every time I see something new from Robert Hernandez, it's like a blow to the head! In a good way! His work floors me." The influence of Hernandez, who is known for his black and gray realism, is apparent (page 37) in pieces such as Dan's interpretation of Jack Nicholson's character from Stephen King's "The Shining."

Painting by Dan Henk

38), the brightness of the light shining through the window is rendered with simple black and grey. In his eerie "Reanimator," (page 38) as well, we see a haunting glow, both in the man's flesh, which appears to be lit from behind, and in the green substance flashing in the needle.

HIS LIFE TODAY

Despite all the tragedies that have stricken Dan in recent years, he's happy with the life he's created for himself. He now works in Long Island, and he enjoys the proximity to New York City. He explains, "I left Washington, D.C., because I wanted to further my art career. New York is the art capital of the world, so it was a natural choice for someone looking to get serious about art. I get tired of it sometimes, but if I'm away too long, I miss it."

While there are many good points to being a

Painting by Dan Henk

He also credits Benjamin Moss as one of his teachers. He has some tattoos by Benjamin on him, and he explains, "Watching Benjamin Moss tattoo me and asking plenty of questions was a great lesson. A good artist will always have something to teach you if you just stay attentive. If I'm around a tattoo artist I respect, I keep my eyes and ears peeled, and I'll always learn something."

He also cites illustrators John Harris and Donato Giancola as influential in his own development. He explains, "I saw the way John Harris, the commercial illustrator, used form and tone to create the illusion of mass, and I like the way Donato Giancola uses texture and color to render images with an almost translucent glow."

Dan achieves similar effects in his own tattoos. In his portrait of a soldier, for instance (page tattooist in New York City, Dan also suggests that it's a city that might be a little oversaturated with tattooists. "People can be a little closed-minded and cliquish," he explains. Tattooing was illegal in New York City for several decades, which has lead to a strong underground feel to the tattoo community in the area. It's like a big family if you are an insider, but it can be a difficult city to crack if you arrive from the outside. Despite these drawbacks, Dan loves the diversity. He says, "With such an immense population, you really encounter all kinds of people. Tattoos are much more accepted in New York City than other places. I notice the difference whenever I travel to a more rural area. It's amusing the reactions I see. You would think that people had never seen a tattooed person before. If nothing else, at least New York has a very vibrant scene. There is always plenty to do."

Dan has a unique approach to applying the business to his tattoo art. He believes that if he does work he's passionate about, his name will get around and his business will grow. He explains, "If I were a better businessman, I would be much richer...but then again, if it was all about the money, I'd work on Wall Street. I try to be reasonable with the cost of these tattoos. I work with

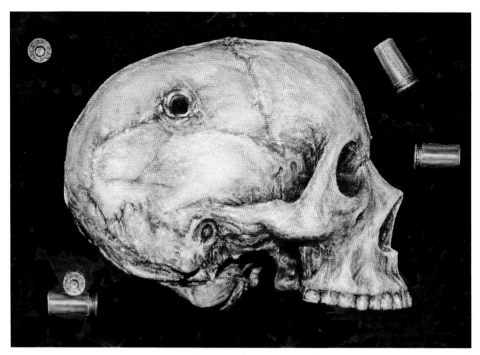

Painting by Dan Henk

Dan Henk at work

Painting by Dan Henk.

Dan Henk at work.

people so we can achieve a cool image that isn't dependent on their budget. If my customer is concerned about cost, I ask what he or she is looking to spend, and we work something out, or in rare cases, I turn down the piece. Price shouldn't be a factor in how the end product looks." He believes that the best form of promotion is the work that he puts out on his clients, and relies largely on word of mouth to spread the message about his work. "I try to focus on work I can really bury myself in," he says. "I look for images that tell a story, that I can get lost in…That helps me get lost in the artistic process and not worry about inconsequential things like time."

When Dan isn't tattooing, he practices mixed martial arts. He began his martial arts career 15 years ago with Tae Kwon Do, in which he holds a second degree black belt and won the gold medal for the State of Virginia in 1994. As he got older, he began to explore other martial arts, including Brazilian Jujitsu, Jeet Kune Do, and Muy Thai Kickboxing. He is also working on a novel, which he was inspired to write after working with novelist Wayne Simmons in promoting his work. He keeps himself busy with various art projects as well, including a recent gig for Madcap comics as a political cartoonist. His other interests are diverse, and he explains, "I go to concerts, mountain bike, shoot guns…you know…normal stuff!"

HIS FUTURE

Dan plans to keep tattooing, as he finds the constant influx of work to be inspiring. "It changes you over time. You evolve. You develop as an artist. What seemed to be a great idea or the best avenue to travel down mutates into something totally different as you grow and change."

He says he sees himself growing and changing, and he believes it's a good thing: "I just want to constantly grow. Once you stop, you die. I remember reading a very depressing interview with the illustrator Bernie Wrightson years ago. He stated that after he illustrated his famous Frankenstein pages, he knew he would never reach any further heights. He essentially gave up. He backed off, and nothing he has done since has approached the quality of the earlier work. I wouldn't ever want to be like that. I don't feel like I've reached a plateau yet. I learn something new almost every day, and I want to keep it that way!"

Dan often works with horror characters, such as this rendition of Pumpkinhead.

Dan's interpretation of Pumpkinhead.

IN HIS OWN WORDS: DAN HENK Q&A

Q: Do you believe that you are a part of a particular style? Or do you think your style is part of a particular movement in tattooing?

A: Well, realism. I like the flow and color scheme people like Guy have brought to tattooing, and I like the personal touch of people like Robert Hernandez. I wouldn't say I'm part of a movement exactly, but I am pursuing a unique, realistic outlook. There are others who are doing something similar, such as Paul Acker, Robert Hernandez, Joe Capobianco, Nick Baxter, Jeff Ensminger…there are plenty of others, all at the same time doing the same thing, but with their own unique styles.

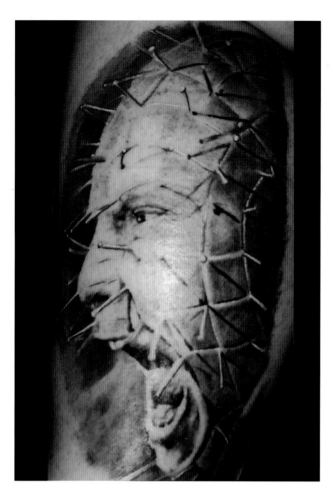

Dan's vision of Pinhead.

Q: *What do you think of the tattoo industry today?*

A: People complain all the time about too many artists working now and how different it is from the good old days. I think the changes are great, though. I think the technology from machines to needles and inks is better now than ever. The artists increase in skill and ability every year, and society as a whole has grown much more accustomed to tattoos in the culture.

The bar has certainly been raised. Kids are getting out of art school and heading straight into tattooing. That never used to happen. Expectations are much higher as well. There are painting seminars at tattoo conventions now!

There are always way too many bad artists out there, and the basic tools of the trade are unfortunately available (in a poor quality form) to every idiot with a few hundred dollars. But overall, how can you possibly look at the work done 10 years ago and the work done now and not see an improvement?

It sucks that tattooing is being co-opted by the boring generation of dimwitted social butterflies. They already had their go at Punk Rock, churning out all the Blink 182s and Good Charlottes, but I'd rather look at the glass as half full instead of half empty. I see better work than ever nowadays.

Q: *Do you travel much to tattoo?*

A: I go to maybe six shows a year. That might be a lot to some, although people like Larry Brogran probably do twice as many! I think shows can be an important influence. They allow the artist to get feedback on his or her work, interact with other tattooists, and reach the gen-

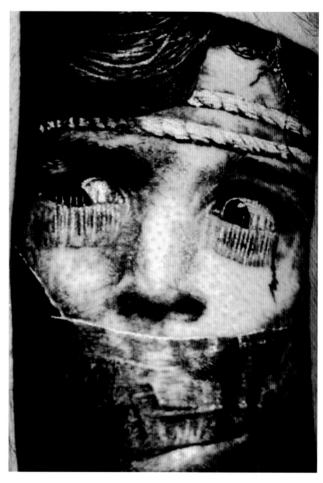

Notice the details and textures that Dan captures with black and gray tones.

eral public in a forum that's just not available at the home shop. Not to mention, of course, that the media never hurts!

Traveling outside your home city is a great chance to expose your work to future clients that otherwise would not have heard about you. I get a lot of work from out-of-state clients, and I think making myself visible to a range of different people plays a large part in that.

My favorite convention, hands down, is Durb Morrison's Hell City show. It's expertly run from open to close, and it's geared toward the artist with custom trophies designed by Joe Capobianco. They have great events all day, and it has a great feel. Running close on Durb's heels are the Amsterdam and Stockholm conventions.

Q: Do you have a favorite tattoo that you've done?

A: It always changes. I can tell you some of my favorites. I tattooed a fetal skeleton in a liquor jar (page 38). I was really happy with the image I drew up, and I thought it was a great idea for a tattoo.

I also really like my rendition of Jack Nicholson from "The Shining." It's a great movie, and I felt like I accomplished what I set out to with the piece.

It might sound a bit pretentious, but I'm always really hoping that my new favorite will be coming up any day. I've grown more

A tribute to the film "Hellraiser"

A chestpiece inspired by Geiger.

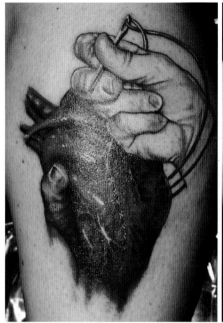

To create eerie effects, Dan zooms the focus here on the heart and hands instead of presenting an entire scene.

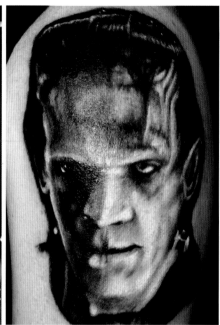

This is Dan's version of Dr. Frankenstein's monster.

The clever addition of a thought bubble makes this tattoo interesting.

selective with the tattoo projects I take on, and I try to dedicate myself fully to each new piece.

Q: What was it like being Dan Henk growing up?

A: I grew up all up and down the East Coast, but I wouldn't really call anywhere home. Newburg, New York, was where my neighbor's son bashed in another kid's head with a baseball bat. I lived on the military base in Fort Bragg, North Carolina, and played soldier using fireworks as weapons among the old, abandoned World War II training fields in the woods. I lived in white trash Southern Florida, where I got into metal, started smoking, and made it around town on a bicycle. I lived in downtown Washington, D.C., amid

Painting by Dan Henk.

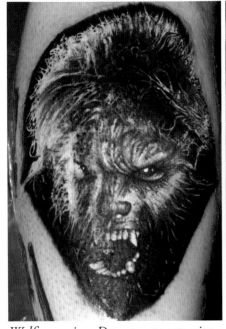

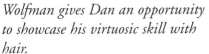
Wolfman gives Dan an opportunity to showcase his virtuosic skill with hair.

A zombie.

Dan calls this the "Bad Wife" tattoo.

the squalor of a minimum-wage job washing dishes, drinking 40s, and exploring abandoned housing projects. Just normal kid stuff.

Q: Do you have some memorable stories of unusual clients?

A: Well, I have this one client who probably takes the cake as far as being memorable. He has stick figure strippers tattooed on him. He picked incessantly at the tattoo, and when questioned about the scabs, he would tell people the strippers were infected…not the tattoo. He had me tattoo a zombie chasing a carton of soy milk on his inner arm. I also did some more straightforward tattoos on him, like a zombie in boxer shorts barbequing a hand and foot on a grill, and a zombie geisha eating a finger like a French fry.

I have another customer who had me tattoo the image off "April Fool's Day" on his forearm. It's the back of a woman, her hand is raised with a champagne glass…but tucked behind her is a knife. He said it was in memory of his ex-wife.

I had another guy get a tattoo of a woman with a blade through her head with the words "Who is this under my knife?" encircling it. I

A dramatic portrait of a woman.

47

Blood splatter contrasts with her smile.

Vivid greens make Dan's swamp creature striking.

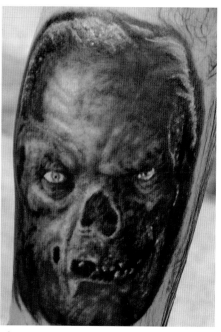

A monster.

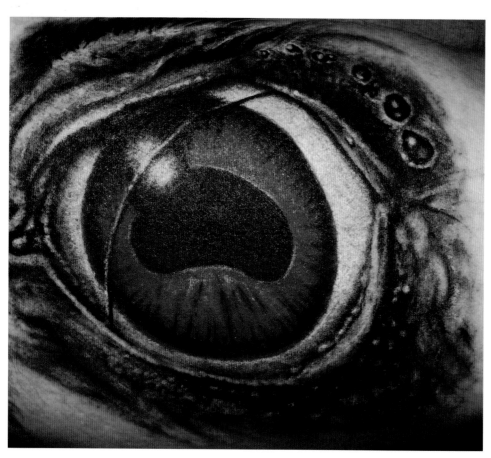

A creature's eyeball.

could actually keep you here all day with endless stories…I don't tend to tattoo the most normal clients.

Q: Do you remember you first tattoo?

A: It was on my ex-girlfriend. I "reworked" a mediocre tattoo she had gotten at the New York City tattoo convention. Let me tell you how much that tattoo sucked! I broke up with her before I ever had a chance to fix it up for her. I still regret it—the tattoo. Not the breakup!

Q: Do you think your art has gone through many phases, or have you always stayed true to your vision?

A: I've gone through plenty of stages.

Tattooing has affected my painting, and vice versa. I've evolved away from attempting to manipulate insane detail into every piece, toward working with the contrast and lighting to hopefully make the picture pop. I've changed my mind over what works as a tattoo way too many times.

Sketchiness and abrupt endings might work well for an illustration, but I've found they can ruin an otherwise good tattoo. I've narrowed my palette, using fewer colors but more shades—it's all in an attempt to capture a mood.

I've also been incorporating more photographic effects, singling out a detail or feature and letting the background fall out of focus. Over time, I've learned to pay more attention to the flow of the body. The best tattoos don't just look good on paper. They glide well with the skin and

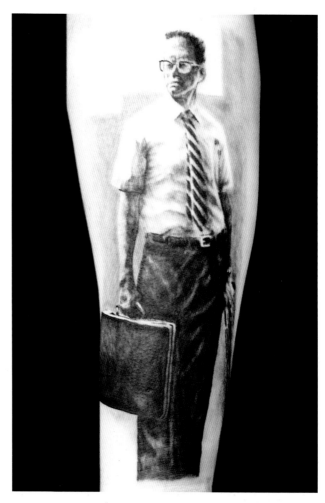

A still from the film "Falling Down".

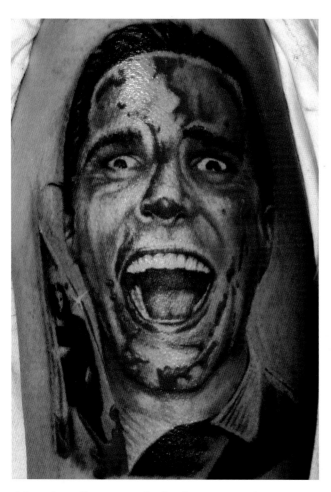

Note the reflection in the knife.

subcutaneous contours, complementing the overall look. And, I've learned to turn down images that just won't work! Every tattoo you do has your name attached to it. If I don't think I can pull it off, I will pass.

Chapter Four

Sean Herman

Tattooing's Hopeless Romantic

One of the most exciting young artists tattooing today is Sean Herman. He's currently unaffiliated with any shop, and Sean likes it that way. He's always been a bit of a drifter, and having the freedom to live like a nomad is one of the great advantages to a tattooing career.

Beyond the flexibility the profession has granted Sean's lifestyle, however, is his contribution to the industry. His deep respect for the art, his refreshing attitude, and his rapid ascension in skill

Sean Herman tells us that living life is his art.

have made him one of the most interesting artists, and his contributions to the tattoo Renaissance are still evolving.

His Early Career

It was the summer of 2003, and young Sean Herman was working as a handyman in a small-town Mississippi flea market. He'd been wandering around the Southeast for a few years, trying on various lives and livelihoods, and nothing seemed to fit. He'd tried out the ministry, attempted college, and even found himself homeless for a stint, sleeping on park benches in the Birmingham, Alabama, area. At this point in his life, Sean truly was a lost soul.

One afternoon in Mississippi, however, he received a phone call from his destiny. He had met tattoo artist Kele Idol a few years before at Aerochild Tattoos in Birmingham. While getting his own tattoo, Sean expressed an interest in learn-

In the blues in this chest piece, there are echoes of Brandon Bond's trademark blue faces, but with a unique Sean Herman interpretation.

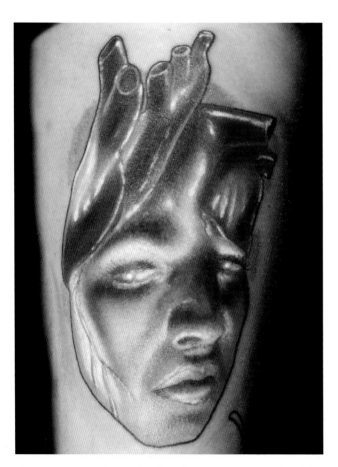

Elements of Josh Carlton's style may be found in this eerie piece by Sean.

ing the art form. Kele was unable to take on an apprentice at the time, but when he was ready, he tracked Sean down and invited him to return and study the indelible art. Sean jumped on the opportunity.

Sean became interested in tattooing as a boy. He remembers watching a National Geographic special about the history of tattooing, and he explains, "After I saw it, I knew. I wanted tattooing to be my life." He'd also been interested in punk rock as a teenager, so the omnipresent ink on his music idols' arms added to the mystique of the art in his mind.

Since finally finding his entrance to the industry through the folks at Aerochild, Sean has made a name for himself as one of the most talented young artists on the scene. In the ensuing five short years, he has been recognized at several tat-

The grotesque exposed teeth and gums create a disconcerting effect in this portrait.

too conventions for his whimsical style, his use of bold colors, and his commitment to growth in his own work.

Sean credits Kele Idol and Aerochild's owner Justen Kontzen with allowing him to get a food in the door of the tattoo world, which can be difficult to enter. He explains, "They taught me how to put in a solid tattoo, but like any artist, I wanted to expand my tattooing. I decided that I needed to start traveling and learning from others." Excited by the opportunity to work with some of the most well-known artists in the industry, he began doing guest spots at Brandon Bond's *All or Nothing* in Atlanta, Georgia. This soon paid off when Bond offered him full-time work.

After tattooing for just a year and a half, Sean found himself working with some of the best artists in the industry, including Bond, Zeke Owens, and Josh Carlton. He learned the ins and outs of how to promote yourself and your art via *All or Nothing's* marketing machine, Sean got his name and his artwork some recognition early in his career.

HIS STYLE

He also had the opportunity to work with artists who were pushing the edge of tattoo possibility, and his art blossomed during this period. He soaked it up like a sponge.

The influence of the artists he worked with at *All or Nothing* is evident in his work. In the beautiful blues and graceful color blends, for instance, we see echoes of Brandon Bond. In the ghostly hues he creates in some of his portraits, are hints of Joshua Carlton's unearthly color schemes and figures.

Wherever the influence of another artist is apparent, however, Sean's unique style still shines through. He

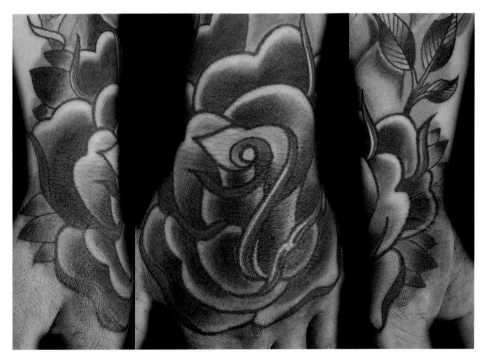

A Traditional American-style rose.

imbues Bond's blues with an ethereal quality, heightening the beautiful and translucent effects over the morbid. He takes Joshua Carlton's chiaroscuro and soft shading, and pairs it with bold red and the grotesque frame of an anatomical human heart (page 51). He has learned well from his teachers, and he has emerged from his schooling with a strong artistic flavor of his own.

Sean is humble about how rapidly his star has risen as an artist, explaining, "I still feel like I am an apprentice. I'm still the student. I think I'll be in this apprenticeship for a long time. Every time I'm around a new artist, I learn something new. I store it in my bank. I still have so much to learn."

When asked what he thinks makes his tattoos stand out as unique in the industry, Sean says he has a hard time viewing his portfolio objectively. He explains, "I try to always change and always grow, so I'm always doing a variety of new things. I think my work always looks completely different. From the illustrated to the more traditional, I'm always trying to change. The one thing that I've heard consistently, though, is that the emotion in the pieces I tattoo is consistent. I hope it's true."

The rays of light beaming from this heart recall the sacred heart image common in religious iconography.

It is true that Sean's style is perpetually evolving. From more traditional pieces, with the bold outlining and straight black shading we identify as quintessentially American tattooing, to more avant garde and experimental images, the one thing that resonates in his work is the element of pathos.

Perhaps because he is young, it is easy to look through Sean's portfolio and witness various phases in his evolution. When he hits on a technique that works, he will include that approach through a series of tattoos, and then move on to another technique after a few applications. He explains,

Sean juxtaposes traditional tattoo imagery with cutting edge techniques to achieve surreal effects.

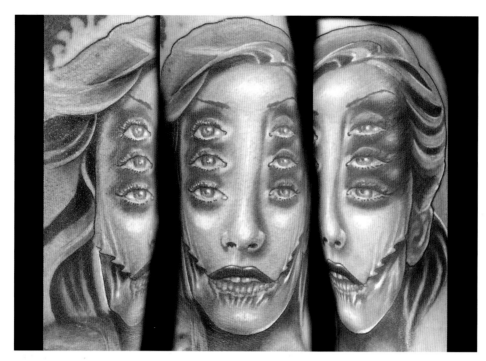

The combination of realism and horror in some of Sean's tattoos creates some shocking effects.

Crab-rose hybrid.

"Once I started doing the tattoos that I really felt were an extension of myself, the phases in my work became more obvious. I had a point where I did everything in really weird, random color schemes…They weren't weird and random to me, but to others, they seemed strange. I had a point where I did weird hair, kind of in the style of Alfonse Mucha, on all the girls I tattooed. Then there were other bits I'd add, like traditional elements, or teeth, or filigree. I feel now that I'm trying to combine all of these things that I've used throughout my 'phases' to create cohesive pieces that have their own look and style."

If a Sean Herman tattoo were to be picked out of a lineup, it might be because of the bold colors or the odd thematic configurations, but more likely it would be because the tattoo conveyed a soft sense of melancholy (pages 52 & 53). His style is marked less by technique and more by pathos.

HIS PRESENT CAREER

While he appreciates all he learned about tattooing and the exposure he got from *All or Nothing*, Sean eventually parted ways with the Atlanta powerhouse. "I let Brandon know a year and a half in advance that I would be leaving," he explains. "I decided I wanted to travel and learn from other artists again. When I left, I traveled for more than nine months, learning from every artist that I admired and loved."

Working in the spotlight helped Sean realize that it wasn't right for him, and he began to reflect on what he wanted to achieve as an artist as well as a human being. He says, "I've completely changed my approach to everything. Now, my priority is to get information out to people. If people are going to look at what I'm saying and doing, I'd better be doing something good, you know? I guess that's what one of the biggest lessons of working somewhere like All or Nothing was for me. It was a big influence on my career, but kind of in the opposite way that people would think. I didn't want to create an empire, but to destroy one."

Sean has since begun to include more than just his artwork and his newest tattoos on his website. He had begun to tire of the promotional aspects of tattoo work, and he now regards his role as an artist in society as a catalyst for change. He now includes other information in his promotions, such as videos, movies, music, thought, and links to ideas that he finds influential in his own evolving personal philosophy. "When I first started," he says, "I pushed all my personal beliefs aside to succeed, and I was wrong for that. I spent a lot of time doing magazine mail outs, Internet work, advertisements—all of it. But really, I hate business. I'm not a business guy. I can tell you all day long what you should do for your business to succeed, but I don't want to do it. When it comes down to it, I hate capitalism. It's failed, and it's creating more and more pain with every breath, with every product sold. So that being said, my way of handling promotion has changed quite a bit."

During the nine months that Sean spent on the road, he toured Detroit, Michigan; Gothenberg and

The hair in this portrait is reminiscent of Art Nouveau style.

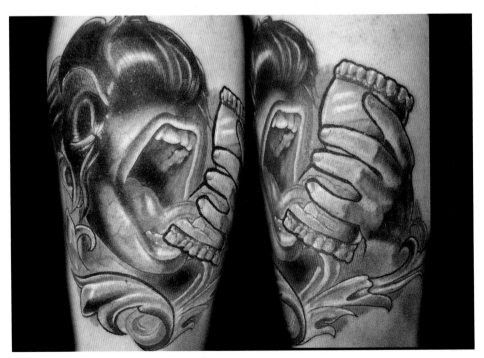

Teeth-time monster—the influence of Surrealist art is clear here.

The translucent skin color in this piece makes it beautiful despite the horror theme.

This is Sean's version of Eve.

The perspective is intensified in this piece.

Stockholm, Sweden; Amsterdam; San Diego, San Francisco, Los Angeles; various places in Mexico; Calgary, Canada; Columbus, Ohio; Philadelphia, New York City, Long Beach, Brooklyn, Niagara Falls; Virginia, the Appalachian Trail, the Gulf Coast; Pensacola, Florida; and several other cities. He had planned to land finally in San Diego where his friend Craig Driscoll works in a private studio; however, he was waylaid due to his mother's diagnosis with cancer. He lived with her in Birmingham to help with her care for a while, and now has landed at Royal Street Tattoo in Mobile, Alabama.

While he has enjoyed traveling, he hopes to find some balance and to slow down. "The problem with traveling so much," he says, "is how much time you spend alone. I've spent countless nights in a bar or coffee shop, reading my book, alone. When you do meet people, it's for such a short time that it is difficult to form real relationships with them. Maybe I'm just getting old, but I'm ready to settle. I still want to travel and see my friends, but not the way it's been. I want a home."

HIS BACKGROUND

Sean's nomad lifestyle began early in his childhood. He was born in Geneva, Illinois, but before he was eight years old, he had lived in Portland, Oregon, and Vancouver, Canada. His family sold everything they had and relocated to an Indian reservation for a while, and then they lived with his grandmother in Wisconsin. From there, they moved to Minnesota, and when his parents split up, he moved with his mother to St. Paul. When his mom remarried, they headed South, and finally settled in Alabama, where he grew up in Daphne, which he describes as one of the most beautiful places he has ever seen.

When he was a teenager, Sean found himself compelled to study religion. He wasn't raised to be religious, but he began preaching Sunday sermons, doing missionary work, and contributing to many Christian festivals and events while in high school. When he started college at Samford University in Birmingham, however, he began to question his religious beliefs, and was disappointed that he couldn't find anyone to answer his questions to his satisfaction. He realized that he could no longer continue down the ministerial path, and he parted ways with his church. He still counts this time in his life as being influential on his personal philosophy and his artwork, and he enjoys incorporating religious iconography into his artwork.

THE FUTURE

Sean believes that he has come into his own as an artist at this point, and he is eager to see what is coming next in his own creative evolution. He says, "At first, I felt like things had to look a certain way. My art was stale and had no impact. I was just trying to create something that I thought looked good. I took a step back and looked at my life, and I wasn't happy." He has since taken the focus off of production and put it back on living his life, and he has recognized a change for the better in his art. "My art follows my desire and drive," he explains. "As I grow and become happier in my life, so does my art!"

The stylized hair here recalls Traditional American work, but the realism in the skin tones is pure post-modern tattooing.

Sean includes Traditional American-style wings in this photorealistic piece.

IN HIS OWN WORDS: SEAN HERMAN Q&A

Q: *Do you remember anything about the first tattoo you ever did?*

A: The first tattoo I ever did was a logo for a record label called *No Idea*. I think the band Against Me! was using it as their logo at the time. The tattoo was on the piercer at Aerochild, this guy named Matt-O. Surprisingly, the tattoo went really well. It was a solid black little monkey head. I wasn't nervous for some reason. I just attacked it, went for it, and did it. Now all the pieces that came after it were a different story! I definitely

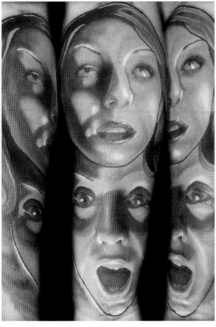

The glowing red-and-orange background of this piece gives the effect of a setting sun.

Wild color combinations are frequently found in Sean Herman's work.

This is a modern take on a classic theme.

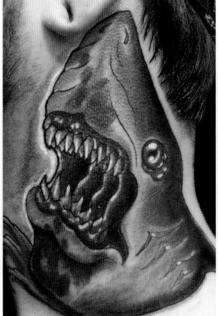

The skull appears to be glowing from within.

Here, the shark is placed on the neck to flow with the body's natural musculature.

Glowing eyes illuminate this image of a classic grim reaper.

wasn't hitting them out of the park at that point…I wasn't even hitting them!

Q: Who were some of the artists that you looked to for inspiration early in your career, and whom do you admire now?

A: Early in my life, I looked up to comic book artists the most. I loved Mike Alred, who drew Madman and X-static. He had a clean, almost pop art style that was still really dark and strange. I think he might be one of my strongest influences. I also admire Guillermo del Toro. He is probably my greatest influence, hands down. When I watched his movies, I was overwhelmed. He creates an entire world that you are living in with him for the duration of the movie. That's what I want to do with my own art…I want to create a world that you feel like you are observing and becoming a part of. His use of the grotesque with the beautiful is absolutely amazing. His creatures move like dancers, with this beautiful flow, even right down to their finger movements. I've always wanted to create my own world and then show it to everyone else. Most tattooists probably list their influences as other tattooists, and tattooists have definitely influenced me…but for the core of where my art comes from, it's those two. Always has been, and always will be.

Rose-hair lady.

Q: Do you remember when you decided to pursue tattooing as a career?

A: I realized that it was all I wanted to do. I was washing dishes one night at a Japanese place where I was working. In my down time, I had drawn all over this Styrofoam cup…completely covered it! I loved every minute of it. I was trying to create pictures that flowed naturally with the shape of the cup, the contours, and the overall roundness of it. Every time dishes came back for me to clean and I had to

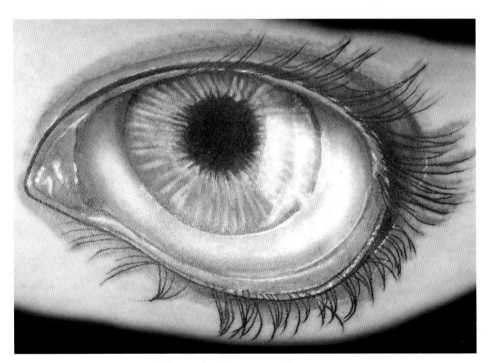

The details in the iris of this eyeball are astonishing.

Sean illustrates his surreal take on the skull, a classic tattoo theme.

Sean combines several common themes of Traditional American tattoos, making this piece uniquely his.

stop, it was like I was taken out of my world and thrown back into the labor force. I hated it. At that point, I decided to take complete control of my life. I made a promise to myself that I wasn't going to have any more jobs like that one. I didn't want to work for someone, doing something that I didn't love with all of my heart. Life is only so long, and we only have so much time, and I was going to take advantage of every second, starting right then.

Q: You've mentioned that you hate business. How does the work of tattooing intersect with the creative aspects for you?

A: I hate business…Despise it. I think business is ruining a beautiful art and industry at this point. Huge corporations are trying to wiggle their way into our art form…this art form that has been passed down for thousands of years…just to make a dirty buck. F—- that. I want no part in it. It's disgusting. They are trying to sell something that is personal and beautiful and make it commercial and disgusting. They are lying to good tattooers, telling them that they can earn some money, get their names out there, and retire early. In reality, these businesses are destroying the artists. They use them for who and what they know and then dispose of them like a used piece of toilet paper.

We all have to make a living, but we don't have to pillage and bastardize this beautiful art. Yes, I do charge for a tattoo, but I think that tattooers need to take a step back and realize how this over-saturation is really going to affect the industry we are in.

Q: What about your family life? How does it intersect with this career?

A: I don't have much of a family life at this point. I'm single, so I don't have the relationship-type situation. I do help out with the care of my Mom and stepdad since she's been diagnosed with breast cancer. I've been spending the majority of my time lately with her trying to figure out what we can do and really trying to make whatever time she has left good.

I used to be a workaholic, and I lost a lot because of it. I lost a marriage and my sanity. I thought that if I just succeeded a little more, if I just did a little more and pushed a little further, it would make me happy. The truth is, it didn't. That is where my friends and family became more important to me than ever. It was like waking up from a haze—an extended dream—and realizing everything I had neglected. I had put my work before everything, and because of those choices, I lost everything. I've been building that back up these days, making my friends and family my focus. Everything else comes after.

You know, I used to spend all my time wishing

Hear no evil. See no evil. Speak no evil.

Neo-traditional style roses.

I could do certain things, wishing I had the time. Now, I do it. I think that tattooing shouldn't be a job…it should be something you love to do. The second it becomes work, you're overworking yourself and doing too much. You have to take time to step back and get everything into perspective, to make sure you're doing what you want to be doing and accomplishing everything you've ever dreamed. That has to be the focus.

Q: So what do you like to do besides tattoo?

A: I like to live! I know it sounds funny, but I tell people that living life is my art. Some people paint, and some people draw…I want to live every second to the fullest. I'm a hopeless romantic. I want to go out and do everything I've ever wanted to do. I love this world so much that I really want to make a difference. I've tried to change the focus of everything in my career to education. I'm fortu-

This is Sean's take on Medusa.

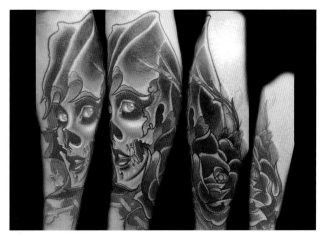

A female grim reaper.

Sean's take on a werewolf.

A female mummy.

nate that people care what I have to say and check out my website all the time. Because of that role, I really want to have something to say and to try to make a positive difference for everyone.

We're living at a bleak time in the world. Poverty is up, we're bombing people, and we're destroying the land we live on. It's difficult for a lot of people to get out of the bubble we're living in and see what's going on…

We live in a world of screens. We wake up in a house covered in windows, screening us from the morning light. We drive our cars with windows screening us from the other drivers, so we don't have to make eye contact. We work in cubicles that separate us from each other, so we have minimal interaction. We hunger for connection, touch, compassion, but we fear to show it and give it to others. We need a change—a revolution! It doesn't have to be this way. We can live the way we've always dreamed and do anything we want, if we just do it!

Q: *So what do you propose?*

A: We need to get educated on what is really going on around us. There is a reason America is the most obese nation, the most depressed nation, and the richest nation. We need to take a stand and tell the governing officials that we aren't going to take it. We need to tell the corporations that we want no part in their poisoning of our families, our children, and our world.

We need to learn where the wool is being pulled over our eyes. That's where education comes in, and it's my focus more than anything now…more than tattooing and more than art. My focus is on change.

Q: *Do any of your clients stand out as particularly memorable?*

A: They all mean something to me, but one that stands out is one I did on a young guy. His brother had just passed away, and he wanted to get a portrait of him tattooed on his chest. When they looked for a picture to use, the family realized that they didn't have any pictures for me to use as reference. His brother came to me with a tiny picture that was all they had, and he was in tears over it. I agreed to do the tattoo.

It was definitely a very difficult tattoo to do. When we were finished, he stood up to take a look at it. He looked in the mirror and was silent. I thought, "Oh man, this can't be good. He then started to cry. He said that it looked just like his brother, and that he loved it. We both got choked up and teary eyed. We hugged and went our separate ways, but I'll never forget that day.

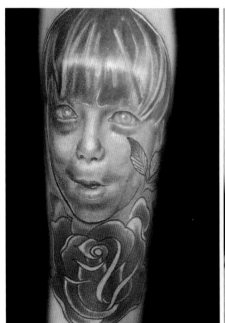

Portrait with a rose.

Half-sleeve portrait with rose.

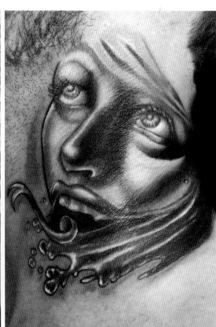

A neck portrait.

Chapter Five

Shannon Schober

Tattoo as Sculpture

For every tattooist, the human body becomes a blank canvas. Instead of paper or velum, tattooists create their images on skin. Instead of brushes and pens, tattooists' tools include needles and ink. For some tattooists, however, the analo-gy of flesh to canvas, needle to brush is not quite sufficient. The human body is not flat, so the idea of the flesh as a canvas fails to reflect the three-dimensional component of creating an image on a human body. Some tattooists engage

Shannon Schober

with the body's natural contours, utilizing the form and motion inherent in our body's landscape to enhance the art, and seeking ways to use the art to enhance the form as well. Instead of working simply as a painter adorning the flesh-canvas, these tattooists combine elements of sculpture, architecture, and other three-dimensional design, enhancing the body's natural ebbs and flows with the addition of tattooed images. Among the artists who incorporate the human form into their work, Shannon Schober is one of the most committed to this approach. In his work, in fact, the subject matter of the tattoo is often secondary to the way it enhances the wearer's body.

This 18-year industry veteran has seen many changes in the tattoo world. He's traveled quite a bit in his career, settling in Asheville, North Carolina, where he owns his own shop, Vitality Tattoo. He has managed to keep a balance in his career between being aware of what is happening in the industry and embracing positive change while also keeping to himself and developing his own unique style. The result is a distinguished artist with a depth of understanding of the tattoo world and a refreshing, open perspective.

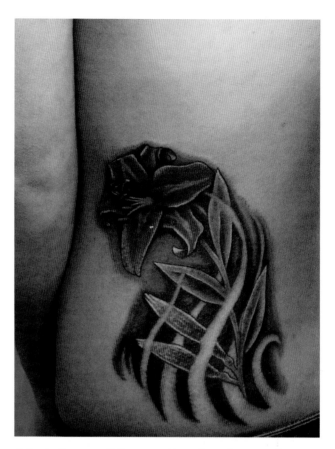

The influence of Georgia O'Keefe is clear in Shannon's large flowers.

BACKGROUND

"I recognized early on that my life must be built on the maximum amount of personal freedom," Shannon says. "I started off making music and making art. I imagined for myself a future of freedom, travel, art, and rocking out." As a teenager, he was active in the D.I.Y. punk scene, and he'd always been attracted to tattoos. When he was 18 years old, his rock star fantasies were interrupted by reality and the birth of his

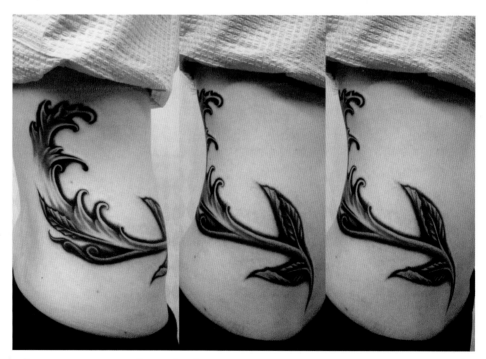

Shannon cites Surrealist Salvador Dali as one of his influences.

This geisha leg piece beautifully sits on the wearer's hip.

time, there was not much tattooing in his small town, and apprenticeships around his state were scarce. The tattoo world was mostly affiliated with bikers, and Shannon did not have a connection to that world.

He got his start with a machine he purchased out of the back of a tattoo magazine which he describes as a "double C-cell battery-powered rotary that looked like half of a chromed soup can with a mechanical pencil coming out of it." He found some friends who were willing to let him experiment, and he learned mostly through the mistakes he made.

He remembers his first tattoo, "We got to the end of it, and there was a fairly recognizable, if somewhat shabby, tattoo of a skull tearing out of my friend's arm. In my youthful ignorance, I was encouraged. In a mutual lack of discernment, I

The lines in this tattoo flow beautifully with the wearer's musculature.

first child. While Shannon knew he would need freedom, creativity, and flexibility in his life to be able to be happy, he also recognized he needed some stability and steady income to support his new family. Tattooing offered that opportunity.

Shannon grew up in Stevens Point, Wisconsin, which he describes as a cultural vacuum. While he found himself often bored as a young man, he is grateful for the lack of stimulation because it helped him get creative in entertaining himself. "I think a lot of kids in my hometown back then were motivated to become artists and musicians," he explains. "We had to make our own scenes."

When he decided to pursue tattooing professionally, he searched around a bit for an apprenticeship, but he found himself shut out. At the kept at it, and my friends kept coming and letting me learn on them."

Eventually, Shannon came across some artists who had completed traditional apprenticeships, and they helped him work through some of his early struggles. He is grateful to Neil Marks of Wisconsin and Miss Kitty Brown of Asheville, North Carolina, among others, for patiently answering his many questions: "I would probably have quit out of frustration if I hadn't had access to these better-trained and charitable artists. I owe much to them for assistance that they may not have even realized they were giving at the time. Being where I am now and looking back, I have to say that I by no means advocate this approach. But hindsight, as they say, is 20/20."

Shannon points to his lack of an apprenticeship as a handicap in hitting his artistic stride,

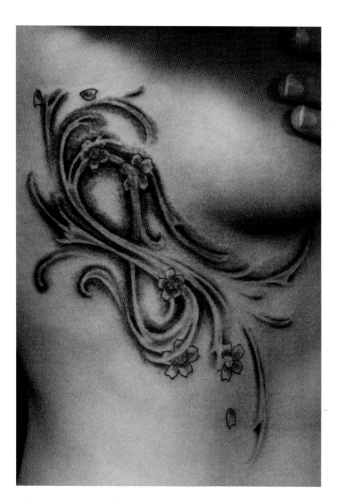

The infinity symbol rendered with water flows beautifully with the female wearer's natural shape.

describing his early work as his "blindly stumbling in the dark as a young, ignorant kid without enough perspective" phase. Once he met some artists who helped guide him to a better place, he began to "unlearn bad habits, pay dues, re-learn tattooing, and work in any licensed street shop that would take me" until he got some solid skills under his belt. In the latter half of his long career, however, he has finally come into his own, achieving a body of work that is characteristically his and working from a solid background and skill set.

HIS STYLE

Shannon cites two of his creative influences as Georgia O'Keefe and Salvador Dali, and there are elements apparent in his work from both artists. He explains, "I've always loved the fact

Cherry blossoms enhance this woman's ribs and draw attention to her curves.

This underwater scene uses negative space to draw the viewer's eye into the tattoo.

to highlight her body (page 66). Shannon strives "to view the aesthetics of the body and its range of motion as equal to, or maybe even as more important than, the imagery I am adding to it. I try not to cover someone up with ink, but to draw the eye into the work with negative space, and to use my composition to draw the eye out of the tattoo and along the curves of the body and the underlying topography of muscle and bone."

In the tribal-flower leg piece (page 66), for instance, the bold, black tribal design flows gorgeously with the wearer's musculature. Shannon softens the masculinity of the tribal work with large, brightly colored flowers. In this tattoo, there is no subject matter other than the wearer. It truly serves as a beautification of her body; it is the tattoo's only purpose.

Shannon finds much of his inspiration in nature.

that an undercurrent of meaning could exist in art and be interpreted differently by the individual. As a kid, those two painters, I think, appealed to me on a subconscious level that I didn't even understand at the time. Now that I see my own work so intertwined with an appreciation of the human form, I've got to laugh at the thought of me as a kid digging all these paintings of big, suggestive, luscious flowers. Georgia O'Keefe made me a little girl crazy, and it has shaped my art ever since."

His work frequently features women as central figures (page 66), as in his striking Geisha leg piece; however, more often, his work features women as central figures in a different sense: the female he is tattooing becomes the subject of the work, and his art serves as a decorative element

Photography by Shannon Schober.

Photography by Shannon Schober.

Photography by Shannon Schober.

Because of his particular eye for the enhancement of the physical form through tattoos, Shannon often works on pieces that are somewhat sexual; however, these enhancements retain an elegance that many tattoos on breasts or lower backs sometimes lose. In his two rib pieces (page 67) that incorporate the wearers' breasts, for instance, he enhances their bodies' natural curves without cheapening the art. It is a rare, delicate balance.

Another influence that has marked Shannon's style is his appreciation for nature. Many of his tattoos feature natural themes (page 68), either as central images or in the background. He explains, "I have always, through the changes in my life, come back to a love for the simple aesthetics found in the natural world. The fact that the human form is just an extension of the wider

Photography by Shannon Schober.

Photography by Shannon Schober.

Shannon found tattooing through the necessities of facing fatherhood at a young age, and this early experience has encouraged him to take advantage of his creative career to build it around a fulfilling family life. As a self-employed small business owner, he has the freedom to plan his own schedule and to choose which projects he will and will not take on. While raising four children, Shannon and his wife have been able to give them many experiences that a more traditional career might not have allowed. "We gave them some variability in their educations with some years of home schooling," he explains. "In an increasingly shifty world, I hope this will help them to think outside the box when they need to."

When he isn't tattooing, Shannon enjoys traveling with his family to be near the ocean. "I

Art by Shannon Schober.

natural world is inspiring. There are echoes everywhere of visual similarities in living and non-living things. Patterns in the way hair grows on the body are similar to the way water swirls around a rock, which is similar to the way a mushroom grows out of a log, which is similar to the way wind blows over a ridge, or the way a fiddlehead fern unfurls. Things like that keep me intrigued in my role of playing with the aesthetics and decorating the human body."

HIS PASSIONS

While tattooing is Shannon's career, he is not consumed by the work. He tries to divide his time between his family, his career, and his other interests, which perhaps contributes to his overwhelmingly pleasant demeanor.

love fishing, snorkeling, and boating, especially in the Florida Keys. We love to travel in and out of the United States and enjoy exploring and learning about new places. I garden, I grow mushrooms, and I make wine. Camping and hiking are also high on my list, and I love food. I enjoy foraging for wild edibles and mushroom hunting."

In addition to tattooing, Shannon pursues oil painting and photography (page 70). "Photography is something I enjoy," he says, "and my clients have become a sustainable stream of models for me to shoot when nature isn't the subject. Oil painting is a freeing release, and I enjoy slapping paint to canvas in a way I could never get away with using a tattoo machine on skin." In both his photography and his paintings, the same themes pervade as are present in his tattoo work: female forms, bold colors cut with black, and nature's beauty.

He also, occasionally, dabbles in guitar, drums, bass, and other, non-traditional instruments. "I enjoy making music from time to time, especially with non-musical items for instruments. I like breathing new life into tired old things that would otherwise end up in a landfill."

HIS BUSINESS

Shannon has been in Asheville, North Carolina since 1999, and it is the home to his thriving tattoo business, Vitality Tattoo. Asheville is a small city nestled in the Blue Ridge Mountains, and Shannon's love of nature brought him there. "In the course of one day, I have seen a bear, an elk, a cougar, and a deer. There are beautiful waterfalls, lots of moss, and abundant nature. That is just awesome to me," he says.

Asheville is known for its creative environment and its fostering of alternative lifestyles. Shannon is grateful for the environment he has found there, explaining, "Whoever you are, you can find your niche here. I am a reasonable drive from the ocean, and the winters are mild. The Asheville Art Museum even put on a great exhibit on tattooing, and I got to hang a little with Spider Webb. This is a great place to be."

As in any town with a diverse, dynamic population, there is some competition in the tattoo crowd, but Shannon says that overall, Asheville's

A hanya mask

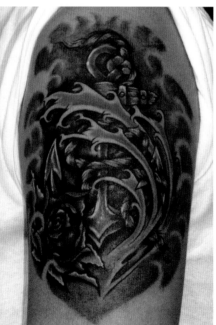

Shannon's interpretation of some traditional tattoo imagery.

Many of Shannon's tattoos feature Asian-inspired imagery.

Shannon's geisha backpiece.

tattoo underground is friendly. "I am constantly impressed by many of the talented artists working around town," he says. "Whatever you are looking for in a tattoo artist, you will find it here. It's a little oversaturated, but I hear that about every town these days."

Shannon thrives on the healthy balance he has established between his zest for living his personal life and the excitement of his career, and it has become a thriving business. He has found a niche where his personal aesthetic, the influence of people in the supportive creative fields, and the demands of his customer base have come together, keeping his work exciting and his business good. His studio has "a very intimate atmosphere with low traffic and a very specific clientele. My shop *Vitality* offers no piercing and no

retails. There is a simple focus on art and experience, placing the business side of things in a supportive role as opposed to being the overbearing consideration."

HIS PHILOSOPHY

If anything has determined Shannon's career trajectory, it has been his commitment to finding his own way. He has come of age as an artist at a time when many artists have been propelled into the limelight as a part of a kind of tattoo Renaissance, and while Shannon has observed these changes and reaped many benefits from the developments in techniques and technology, he has remained committed to his own artistic vision, his family, and his specific approach to his business.

This phoenix enhances the wearer's figure by highlighting her natural shape.

He mentions his respect for others who have taken their own creative paths in pursuing tattooing, and this ideal has served as his guide in his own career. He explains, "One thing that I was disappointed to find in the tattoo scene was a kind of mind-numbing conformity. It seemed to me that people confused the idea of paying respect to the Old School with something ultimately closed-minded. Instead of taking the hard-learned lessons that great artists had laid out in years past and building upon them, many people merely joined a social club with a clichéd aesthetic that was more about patting each other on the back for sticking to tradition. Don't get me wrong…I learned the hard way how important tradition can be, but I find myself loving the art made by people willing to take a risk of not belonging. Hell, not belonging is the original spark of many artists' creativity. Even if my work sucks to someone, or doesn't look the way they expect it should, I would prefer to be able to lay claim to it as something personal, even at the expense of acceptance."

The branches of the tree flow gracefully with the musculature of this woman's back.

IN HIS OWN WORDS: SHANNON SCHOBER Q & A

Q: Tell us about where you grew up. How did your hometown shape you?

A: I'm from Stevens Point, Wisconsin, and I grew up there. I have a love/hate relationship with this place. Being a small, midwestern town, there just wasn't a lot of culture for a weird, creative kid to tap into. My friends and I kind of built our own scenes, but naturally, we were on the fringes. I got beat on a fair amount.

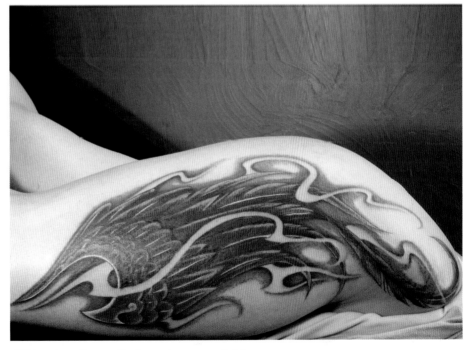

This wing fits perfectly on its wearer's hip.

73

While it sucked, it taught me to persevere in what was important to me in the face of adversity and to take the long view of things. I'd like to see what some of those old tormentors from "back in the day" are up to now. I'm sure there'd be some vindication for me, and some good laughs!

I also learned my love of nature there. Winters were long and ruthless. I hate the cold, so I truly lived the three months out of the year when the snow melted in the springtime and things came to life.

Q: What comes to mind when you recall your most memorable clients?

A: Within the last couple of years, I have had many memorable experiences tattooing soldiers heading to or coming back from war as well as with family members who have lost loved ones to war. This experience is always very humbling. I mean, I draw on people for a living while some people run straight at death for a living. That puts things into perspective for me. I try never to forget it…for all its flaws, this country I live in is a place in which I have ultimate say over the direction in my life. It's something to be thankful for.

Q: Do you have a favorite tattoo?

A: I really like the geisha back piece at the moment (page 72). That one, I think, really captures color for me…the way I see it in my mind's eye. Also, other people seem to love that piece. It's also a great example of what people refer to as my style.

That being said, I have an affinity for many of my tattoos and the way they accentuate the beauty of my clients. I am doing exactly what I want to be doing with my art.

Q: How do you see yourself changing as an artist?

A: I really want to find a balance between cementing and owning my style as perceived by others and moving forward, growing, and redefining my style. I would like this to happen seamlessly as part of a natural progression. I think it can happen gradually over the course of many years to come. At this point in tattooing, I'm a lifer…I've got time.

Q: Do you think some techniques that you use are different from other artists?

A: I like to create bright color schemes but temper them with a lot of black for dramatic

Gladiolas on a foot.

Angel with skull by Shannon Schober.

Phoenix by Shannon Schober.

contrast. Also, a lot of my work plays with layers of dimension and simple symbolism. There is a definite Asian flair to a lot of it as well.

In some of my work, I am willing to use certain textures or "brushstrokes," even if it means some will look past my intent and inaccurately see it as a sloppy, unsuccessful attempt at something else. I really take artistic license as my right, and I enjoy combining styles and themes.

Q: Have you ever felt yourself to be blocked? And how did you get past it?

A: I've experienced many moments of plateau, and there will surely be many more to come. The best thing I've found to get past this is to do anything to shake things up, change my scene. A new medium, new influence, new machine…anything different can serve to point the way forward.

Luckily, also, the client can many times bring a breath of fresh air with a new idea I never would bring to the table. A good new release by a band or musician I admire can help bring me past a sticking point. When all else fails, just relaxing and letting the next wave of inspiration come on its own time will work.

Q: Do you identify with a particular style of tattooing?

A: Not necessarily, although I do feel a kinship with a large group of artists who have brought their careers to fruition as the information age is maturing. The network and promotion made possible by technology has reshaped the tattoo community. Tattooing's overall knowledge base, as well as the outlook of the art itself, has been altered by information technology for many artists who are actively pushing the art and community forward in new ways.

Q: What do you think of the industry today?

A: I love it. I work doing what I love. I have the opportunity to define the nature of my approach and place in the industry. While this freedom also allows many things in the industry that do not appeal to me to flourish, that's the nature of freedom. The positive aspects to be found in the industry far outweigh the negative for me.

Inside Vitality Tattoo.

Vitality Tattoo.

Shannon's shop Vitality Tattoo.

Dragonfly by Shannon Schober.

increasing connectedness, and myriad other variables will play out in tattooing's future. I cannot even guess where it's all heading; I just aim to be as flexible as I can be as these changes wash over us. I intend to do this in one form or another for the rest of my life, even if I have to use it to barter for firewood and chickens. Hah!

Q: Do you travel much?

A: I work the Jacksonville, Florida, show every year, and I plan to add more to my schedule as my children get older. I have done guest spots at many shops on the East coast, and I hope to do more. Traveling is one of my favorite things about being a tattoo artist. Seeing new places and experiencing new things are great for keeping the creative juices flowing.

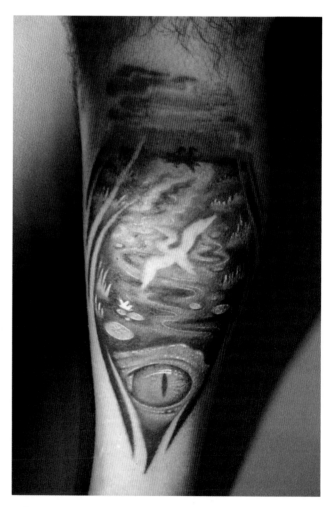

Shannon's interpretation of the Florida everglades.

If something about it bothered me enough to say so here, I'd be doing something to attempt to change it rather than complain, in my own small way. That's what I'm already doing by pursuing my art and my career on my own terms. I see many awesome people in this industry doing exactly the same thing, which is improving the industry overall.

Q: You've had a long career, so you have a unique perspective on the industry. How do you see it changing?

A: I really cannot say. Currently there are many forces outside the industry that will dictate its shape in the near future. These are extraordinary times of potential change. War, climate change, economic instability, globalization,

Tattoo flash by Shannon Schober.

Tattoo flash by Shannon Schober.

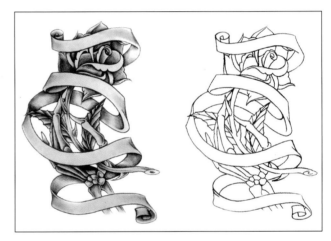

Tattoo flash by Shannon Schober.

Meeting other artists is another great way to grow. Doing work in other people's shops can, if the environment is to your liking, serve to reinforce what you already do similarly in your own shop. By contrast, experiencing things in another shop that you disagree with can further reinforce your personal motivations for doing things differently at home in your own studio.

Tattoo flash by Shannon Schober.

Chapter Six

Matt Griffith

Tattoo's Two Dollar Pistol

"You have to keep pushing to the top," says Matt Griffith of the competition in the tattoo industry. He has come of age as a tattooist at a time many refer to as tattoo art's own Renaissance, which creates a challenging environment in which he thrives. "I will get stoked about my art and tat-toos, but then I open a magazine and see someone else's work that is a whole level above mine. There is always someone better, younger, and hungrier than you, but that is what makes me turn myself up a notch."

Matt Griffith

Matt has not been tattooing for many years, but he has developed a distinctive style that has set him apart in the tattoo world. His funky, cartoon-like images, his unusual source material, and his humble, persistent work ethic have helped him make contacts with some of the best tattooists working today and to launch his own tattoo empire in the small town of Chillicothe, Ohio.

HIS BACKGROUND

Matt was born and raised in Chillicothe, Ohio, where he still lives with his family. He explains, "When I was 17, I thought I hated this hell hole. Now that I'm older, I realize I love it. I have my roots and my family here, and I will always be connected to Chillicothe, no matter where I end up. I've got a lot of pride in this small town and in this area of Southern Ohio. I love it now."

Matt's trademark color work.

Matt juxtaposes New School and Japanese style work.

While he was growing up, Matt remembers staying in trouble for drawing too much. "Whether it was my teacher bitching at me, or my boss when I got out of high school," he explains, "there was always somebody telling me to stop drawing and start working." He found the solution when he realized that it would be possible to turn his passion into a career: "I figured why not make drawing my job?"

Matt got his start as a tattoo apprentice at a local shop in Chillicothe under a guy named Doodle. Matt had gotten a few tattoos himself at the shop, and he asked the owner about how he might get into the business. Doodle offered to help him learn to do things the right way if he remained interested. Matt remembers, "The more work I had done, the more I got interested. In the

A unique take on Traditional American themes.

meantime, I had sent some of my drawings to a magazine, and they got printed. After a few more visits to Doodle, he offered me an apprenticeship."

His apprenticeship lasted for a year and a half, and he began the week of September 11, 2001. "Everyone knows where they were that day," he says. "I was starting my job as a tattoo artist! I think I did my first tattoo about six months after that day. It was a black and gray evil cherub on my own leg." He spent the first year and a half as a tattooist tattooing his own legs with little bits of flash and tattooing his braver friends.

His Style

When Matt first became interested in tattoo art, he was drawn to the black and gray style. "When I started I didn't much like color tattoos," he explains. "Man, did that change! Now, color is what I'm known for."

Many artists experience a similar evolution as they become more educated about what is possible in tattoo art. Before becoming familiar with the cutting edge of tattoo creativity, many of the best tattoos young artists have seen are black and gray. After exploring the tattoo magazines and becoming knowledgeable about tattoos, however, many make the switch to color. Matt's colorful New School work reflects this trend among young artists away from gloomy black and gray toward bright, fun designs.

Matt describes his evolution through several phases, "When I first started, I wanted to do black and gray, and that was it. I just didn't really understand color yet, but once I got the idea of it, I never looked back! Don't get me wrong, black and gray is just as important as color. I just like doing color tattoos. My style had changed a lot, and it's still changing. I was doing a lot of big, cartoony

Traditional American subject matter.

stuff (page 79), and then I moved on to Old School or Traditional, and lately I've been getting into realism and Japanese styles."

The influences on Matt's career, both from tattoo art and other media, have changed as his tastes and style have evolved. As a teenager, he says that Rob Zombie and Bob Ross first inspired him to start drawing: "I used to draw Zombie's art all over my classmates' tablets at school, and then, when I got home, I watched Bob Ross show me how to make the happy little trees." When he started paying attention to the tattoo world, he says, "Jason Goad caught my eye, and also Andy Ringo. His spin on art made me understand that every design I create can have my own spin to it."

Currently, he credits a new generation of artists as inspiration. He spent a few weeks doing a guest spot at All or Nothing while artist Justin Weatherholtz was there as well, and the experience of working with some of the industry's best colorists helped him to fine-tune his own color technique. He says he admires any artist he can learn from, but most often he looks to Kunckles, Giovani, Rich T, Mike Devries, Nikko, Carson Hill, Nate Beavers, and Josh Woods as inspirations.   Recently, he says, "I've been trying to learn

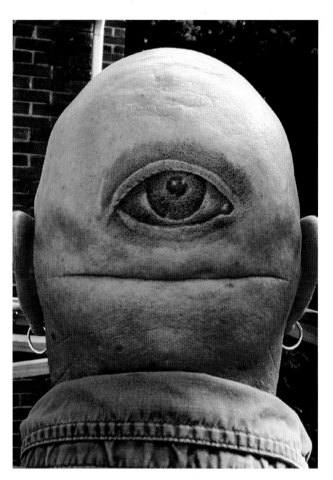

Sherman Prait is one of Matt's favorite clients.

my roots, looking up and reading about the great tattoo artists of the past like Stoney St. Clair and Lyle Tuttle. These are people who opened doors for me, and I want to be educated on my art's background."

The influence of Traditional American tattooing is apparent in Matt's art, both in the themes and techniques he chooses. He says, "I think Traditional American stuff will always be here. It always has been here. I will always hold it close to my heart. It is tattooing. It is the roots. You see an Old School rose or a

Matt working.

This is Matt's take on a pin-up.

A beautiful sidepiece.

Notice the notes rendered with negative space.

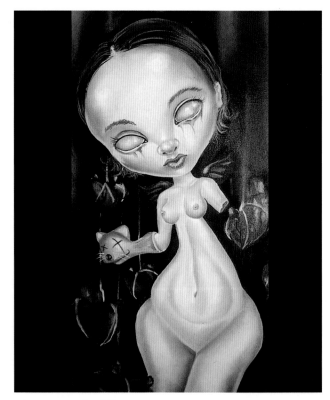

A painting by Matt.

sparrow, and you know it's a tattoo. It doesn't matter if you see it on a T-shirt, poster, sign, or album cover, you know that the style started as a tattoo."

While he reveres the Traditional aesthetic, Matt is not a slave to it. Sometimes artists can become trapped in the historical weight of Traditional American work, but Matt always includes his unique perspective in his designs. He explains, "I think my style comes through. A lot of artists can do any tattoo and do it well, but I try to throw my twist on every piece I do. You know, if you see a Monet painting, you know Monet painted it. If you see a Norman Rockwell, you don't have to look at the name. I want to be like that as an artist. Before you look at the name in the caption in the magazine, you instantly know…that's a Matt Griffith tattoo."

In the last year, Matt has achieved his goal of opening his own shop, Two Dollar Pistol. Before making the leap from artist to business owner, he felt he'd reached a plateau in his creativity. He explains, "I was getting stale, I think, before I moved into my own business. I felt like I was doing the same old thing day in and day out. I wasn't able to get my ideas to skin. When I got my own shop, everything changed. I am growing strong."

Matt's shop sign is a Two Dollar Pistol.

Heart-phoenix hybrid.

HIS BUSINESS

While working at the last shop before he opened Two Dollar Pistol, Matt was frustrated with the lack of security, retirement, and his inability to focus on the kind of artwork he wanted to do in the street shop environment. He'd hoped to open his own shop, and he got his break through a personal tragedy.

Matt's father had told him that if he ever were able, he would help him get set up in business in his own shop. Matt explains, "My dad spent more than half of his life in a factory. He sweat his ass off for me. He worked hard, doing overtime for hours and hours, taking time away from his family, all so I could be happy. My father is my greatest hero. If I am ever half the man he was, I will know that I am doing damn good."

His father passed away recently, and when his mother collected his retirement, she knew that Matt's father would want her to use a part of it to help set him up with his own tattoo shop. Matt says, "I understand how much he had to sacrifice so that I could set up my own shop. When my mom made that gift to me, I went to the busiest street in town and set up shop."

Matt has been pleased with the way his shop has progressed, and he's grateful to his customers for being smart consumers of tattoo art. Even though he's in a small town, he has cultivated a business where he is now doing about 80 percent custom artwork. He says, "They are doing the homework, getting the tattoos they want to get. My customers aren't getting whatever is hanging on the wall and trying to be like every other person. They want something unique."

When Matt's father passed away, he credits his wife and mother as being his lifeline. "We went

Matt's microphone.

The placement of this chest piece accentuates the wearer's physique.

through hell together," he explains. As a man who understands the importance of family, he has chosen to live above his shop. It is even more important to integrate his work and family life now, as his wife gave birth to their first child in April of 2008.

One dilemma he faces as a businessman has to do with working from his home. While living above his shop makes maintaining his family life easy, it is difficult when he is trying to have a day off. He sometimes has to cut off clients who do not understand his need for time with his family. "It is great to be able to get up and go to work without having to leave my home," he says, "but it does make it hard when it's my day off and I want to hang out in the backyard with my wife and baby. It is just a part of being a business owner, though, and I have to be respectful. I understand

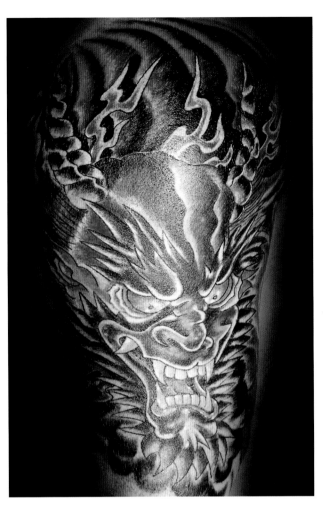

Matt's experimenting with Japanese style artwork.

Matt adds his unique twist to traditional tattoo iconography.

that my clients are the ones allowing me to live this life, and I'm grateful."

With all the excitement of starting a business and becoming a father occurring at once, Matt has struggled sometimes to find balance between his creative life, his family life, and his role as a businessman. "Everything changes when you become a businessman," he says. "You start to feel the stress and the headache of doing everything for yourself. Hell, I don't know what I'm doing, but I do know that this is what I need to be doing."

His wife helps him with the promotional side of his work, which he handles by sending press packets to magazines and uploading as many images of his painting and tattoo art as he can to websites and MySpace. He regards social networks like MySpace as crucial in spreading his name, as

Matt's shop and home in Chillicothe, Ohio.

cool and treat people with respect, and I get respect back."

Matt is also passionate about his painting, which is an avocation he shares with his wife, a talented painter in her own right. He finds it frustrating at times that the business end of tattooing can interfere with his time to paint. "I just don't have the time much anymore, but once in a while I just have to draw something that I just want to draw or to paint something I just want to paint instead of a tattoo that I have to do," he says. "Painting and drawing for myself is important, as it keeps me motivated. It's just my creation and my ideas. It is the purest form of art. You have to do it as an artist. It reminds you why you are here and why you are an artist."

it allows his clients to promote his work as well. "I have a few hardcore clients who will do anything for me," he says. "They plaster my name all over town! They are the ones who keep me open. All my customers are the reason I'm able to do what I love and keep learning something new every day. I'm very grateful."

He has also learned the importance of safeguarding his reputation as an artist and as an upright businessman. No matter what happens in his life, he says it is important to "stay professional. Even when it's hard to be professional, you've got to stay professional. I really care about my name, and I'm learning what works for me is to try to stay one step ahead in the game. If I remember always to stay professional, I keep my

Matt's caption on the cover of International Tattoo Art.

In His Own Words:
Matt Griffith Q &A

Q: Who or what do you credit as being the biggest influences on your career?

A: My family and my friends. To me, they are the same. Without support from my mom and dad, I wouldn't be doing this today. Also, my wife…she was the best thing ever to happen to me. She has helped to mold me and show me how to be a good artist. She keeps me on track and promotes my work on the internet, updating my websites for me. She also loves me and puts up with me, even when I'm stressed and having bad days. When my dad passed away, my wife and my mom were my backbone.

My friends are great, too. They never let me slack off and they show me that I can do these things, supporting me when my life is at its all-time low and making me believe in myself. I

Painting by Matt Griffith.

Painting by Matt Griffith.

would be nothing without my friends and family.

Q: Tell us about your social life. Do you have time for these awesome friends?

A: My friends are truly the greatest. We play video games and shoot guns on the weekends, just sitting around, having a good time, and making fun of each other. My wife and my baby, also…they are my world. Who could ask for a better life?

Q: When you're not involved with your art or business, what do you like to do?

A: Shoot guns, collect guns, reload ammo, read about guns…did I mention I like guns? Remember the movie Tremors? I'm Bert, the guy who thinks the world's going to end and he's going to be safe because he knew it was coming. Yeah, that's me.

Q: Do you have any really memorable clients?

This tattoo is reminiscent of Matt's paintings.

One of Matt's favorite clients.

A: Sherman Prait is the guy who got the eyeball on the back of his head. It's amazing when you meet somebody and you realize that person is just like you. That guy is amazing! I have the utmost respect for him and his family. When I started tattooing him years back, I realized he was a guy who did things the right way. He knows tons more about life than I do, and I try to soak up as much knowledge as I can when I am working on him. He is a part of my family now. You do not have to be my brother to be my brother, you know?

Q: Are there any tattoos that were particularly notable or any stories that stand out?

A: There is not really anything specific that stands out, but I do really enjoy working on older people and the military guys and gals. I get a lot out of working on people that I can learn from. They all share little bits and pieces of their lives with me, and it helps me in my life, like stories from Iraq from the soldiers or life lessons from the old men. People open up a lot when they are in the chair.

Q: Do you have a favorite tattoo out of all that you've done through the years?

A: Really, it changes from day to day. Every time I do a new one and think it's the best, I try to do one better or more crazy the next week.

Q: Because you're talking about changing, how do you think you have changed the most from the beginning of your career? What keeps you motivated?

A: I set goals. I wanted to have a flash set, so I put one together. I wanted to get it distributed worldwide, and then I got that done. I started with the magazines next. I wanted to get my first tattoo in a mag, and I did. Then I wanted to get my first interview, and I made that happen. I did a guest spot at All or Nothing, which was another goal, and then I opened up my own shop. Things are getting checked off my goal list, one by one.

Q: *Do you think your work is changing?*

A: I do see myself changing, and my work. Every day, I grow and I learn. I take pieces of others' work and mix them into mine. I do not steal, but I borrow ideas and add my twist. That's what artists do! I look at the tattoo magazines, and I find what I like. I look at what other people did and try to figure out how they did something, and then in my next tattoo, I try to do it. It keeps me on my toes.

Q: *Are there some techniques that you think are uniquely your own?*

A: I'm not really sure. I like background a lot because I think a tattoo needs to have something behind it to make it stand out. It always makes a tattoo look better. Maybe it's the eyes. I do eyes my way. I think they stand out.

Q: *What are your thoughts on the changing state of the tattoo industry?*

A: Every day, it gets better and more complex.

There are trends, but tattooing is a staple in America, and it's always going to be here. For the rest of time, I believe that people will be getting tattoos. Hell, they are doing tattoos now that ten years ago couldn't be done. New machines, new pigments, new supplies…every day, the industry is evolving and becoming its own.

Q: *Do you make it to many shows?*

A: As many as I can. I really enjoy watching people work. It is a view you can't get from a mag. It lets you see the whole picture, and you can learn a lot from watching a tattoo artist.

Q: *How does the traveling impact your home life? Or your business?*

A: I'm looking forward to finding out! I don't get out too much right now. I want to, though. I want to do some shows and guest spots as soon as I can.

Q: *What show is your favorite?*

A: Hell City, for sure. I can't get into it yet. I have been trying for two years, but if you were not a part of the first show, you can't get a booth. I'm waiting!

A New School tattoo machine

Psychedelic teapot.

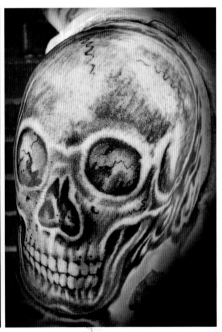
This is a rare black and gray tattoo from Matt Griffith.

Chapter Seven

Chris Thomas

Arkansas' Golden Boy

"Some people like it a lot. Some people don't. All I can say is it is my own custom style," says Chris Thomas of his amped-up color work. "This is what I like, and this is what I do. It is my own form of tattoo expression. I am very happy with where I am as an artist."

Arkansas isn't exactly known for its cutting-edge arts scene, but Chris Thomas has worked hard to develop a tattoo culture there to rival some of the best in the United States.

HIS BACKGROUND

With more than a decade of tattoo experience

Chris Thomas is a New School old-timer.

under his belt, Chris is a New School old-timer. His early career was marked by bad luck, but he persisted in following his dream of becoming a world-class tattoo artist despite his many setbacks.

Chris got his start in a biker-style tattoo shop. He stumbled upon a guy who was looking for an apprentice, and he was excited about the opportunity. He says, "When I showed so much interest, he took it upon himself to show me how to make needles and clean tubes…basically, he showed me the ropes in tattooing."

Like many young artists, Chris got tired of doing the grunt work without any of the glory and he started tattooing out of his house. He experimented on friends and family members, but he eventually became frustrated by the trial and error approach to learning and hoped to find some real guidance by working in a shop. "I was ready for the real world," he explains, "and I wanted a chance to work at an actual tattoo studio."

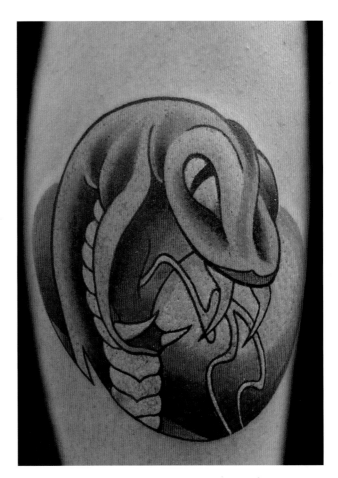

A snakehead with New School flair.

Chris' version of Dare Devil.

He landed a spot at Skinworks in Shreveport, Louisiana, where he worked for about a year. During this time, he had the opportunity to work with the tattooist James Clements, whom Chris cites as being one of the biggest influences on his early career. "In my eyes," says Chris, "James did some really, really awesome work, and he was the first one to show me that designing art for tattoos was so much more than tracing flash off the wall."

At Skinworks, he also learned "a lot about how to work with customers and sell tattoos." Skinworks wasn't the perfect environment for him, but it whet his appetite for bigger, better things than he had thought were possible while working out of a biker shop or tattooing from his house.

The next step for Chris was to relocate. He moved to a shop called Red River, also in Shreveport. He'd learned enough about piercing to feel comfortable at Skinworks, so he started piercing

A neo-Traditional profile.

apprentice him for the six-month period required to become a licensed tattooist. Unfortunately, the woman he worked for had bad intentions. Chris explains, "When it was time to get my license, she decided to get rid of me. She locked me out of her shop with all of my tattoo equipment still in her shop. She demanded that I either pay her $2,500 or work for two more months for free before she'd be willing to help me get licensed. I had to start all over again, and I had to buy new equipment. What a f——r! She needs to learn how to buy her own shit." Although he was frustrated, Chris took it all in stride and set out to find another tattoo shop to apprentice him.

"I was driving down the road one day," he remembers, "and I noticed a new tattoo shop on the side of the road called The Parlor. This shop was pretty well established, and this was a new loca-

Traditional work from Chris Thomas.

full-time at Red River while doing a few tattoos on the side. While most tattooists find their artistic fulfillment in tattooing, there is a lot of money to be made in piercing. Chris says that the combination of extra money and little time spent devoted to his artwork left him a lot of idle time, and he partied quite a bit during his tenure at Red River. "I was kind of going to work to make some money to party, and then I'd do it again the next day," he says. "It was not a good thing…not good for the mind, body, or soul, and of course I wasn't getting anywhere with tattooing, living like that. I wasted a lot of time."

He eventually straightened up, and he decided the next step for him would be to move again. He relocated to Little Rock, Arkansas. At the time, it was difficult to get a tattoo license in Arkansas, and Chris felt fortunate to find a woman willing to re-tion for it. The owner was a guy named Scott Diffie. He looked at the little bit of a portfolio I had with me, and he hired me on the spot!"

The Parlor was a very busy street shop with an emphasis on walk-ins and flash-style artwork. Chris had a chance to test his mettle against a few custom pieces, and he remembers this time in his life as being a kind of coming of age for him. "Scott Diffie is still a good friend of mine," he says. "He helped me out when I was down on my luck. I received my Arkansas tattoo license through him, and I worked for him for about three years. I learned a lot about tattooing and how to work with a wide variety of clientele. There were five other artists at the shop, and they all had very different styles. I learned something about all of the styles of tattooing, and I perfected my line work because I had to tattoo lots and lots and lots of names. It also

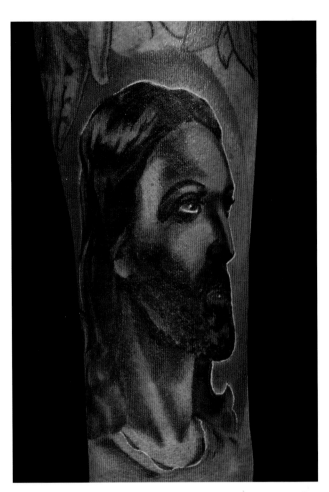

Notice the softer, painterly effects in this portrait of Jesus.

was the first time I had a chance to take regular art and turn it into my own custom piece by tweaking it a little, and I learned how to sell my style to my customers. I took my work to a whole new level at that shop, and I'm grateful."

HIS STYLE

Chris is best known in the tattoo industry today for his unique twist on portrait work. His hyper-colored, intense approach combined with his over-the-top personality has gained him some notoriety in the tattoo world over the last several years. His style has solidified as his reputation has emerged, but he began in quite a different place from where he's arrived today.

He explains, "I have definitely been through a lot of different stages. The first stage I went through I would have to say was the New School sort of tattoo. I really liked the fat outlines, twisted designs,

Here Chris has combined elements of realism and traditional work.

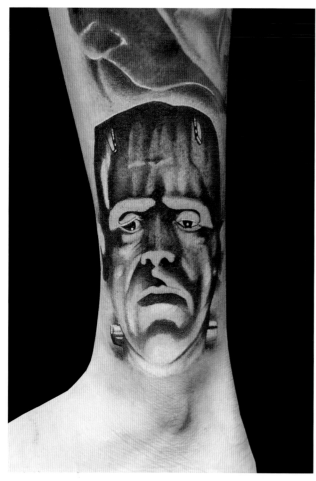

Frankenstein with heightened color.

is less forgiving because you don't have the bold lines to cover up mistakes and crazy designs that make it OK if the tattoo looks twisted up and imperfect. Traditional tattooing doesn't lie. I think the challenge was just what I needed to make me better at that time."

Chris continued with the Traditional American style for a few years until he became interested in tackling portraits. The tattoo industry in general took a turn toward realism and hyperrealism, and Chris appreciated the new art form that was emerging. He didn't simply jump on the bandwagon, however. He continued to incorporate his own taste and style into the hyper-realistic portraiture for which he has come to be known in the tattoo world. "At first," he says, "I started out by mixing my Traditional work in with the faces I was doing…making hard lines and bold colors, and really segmenting the colors in the faces. I heard somebody call that photo-traditionalism one time.

A Bettie Page tribute.

and bold colors in the graffiti-style tattoos. I'd have to say that's how most of my tattoos looked (or tried to look) for the first four years or so of my career." The influence of the New School style is still apparent in his work today, even in pieces that emerge from a different tattoo lineage. Chris tweaks his realistic portraits' perspectives and brightens the colors to achieve some of the surreal effects we associate most closely with the New School movement in tattooing.

His next phase was to explore the Traditional American style, and he experimented with incorporating New School elements to create his own neo-Traditional blended style (page 92). "I tried mixing it up a little, using bold colors instead of the simplified color scheme you usually use in Traditional tattoos," he says. "The Traditional style was a little harder to do than the New School stuff. Traditional

"I am now doing something different, trying to replicate the portrait as realistically as possible. Some of the faces I do have a painterly style or a little more of a comic style. I just play it by ear, doing the style that best suits me to make the project have the look I want."

If one thing marks Chris' style, it is his signature use of color and his attention to detail. "I like to take whatever I am doing and turn up the color volume, making it a little crazy looking," says Chris. "I am also really big into doing detail work, and I try to concentrate on details in the eyes, mouth, and teeth."

HIS BUSINESS

Chris is now the proud owner of Golden Lotus; but Hurricane Katrina marred the path he took to arrive at this point in his career. After nearly losing everything, he found the inspiration he needed to open up his own ideal working environment.

It began while Chris was still working at the Parlor. A friend in the industry invited him to work at a shop in New Orleans during the height of the Mardi Gras season. Chris had never done a guest spot before, and he was excited for the opportunity to travel and to make some extra money. He arrived in New Orleans and went to check out the shop where he'd been scheduled to work. Chris says, "I walked in this shop, and I have to say it was one of the worst tattoo shops I had ever seen in my life. It was a negative experience from the start. The owner handed me a stack of flyers, and he told me to hit the streets and hustle business if I wanted to tattoo, and he told me to find an empty space on the floor and set up my shit. I remember thinking that this guy would never see me again, and I told him I'd just hand out flyers the first day. I'd already rented a room for a few days, so I figured I'd check out a few shops around town to see if there was anyone who could

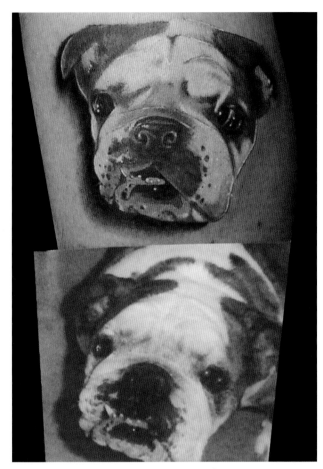

Bud the Dog with Chris's trademark painterly style.

Notice the detail in the lashes.

The stylized hair in this Bride of Frankenstein recalls Chris' interest in Traditionalism.

decided he wanted to move to New Orleans and get a fresh start. He and his girlfriend packed up everything and headed south to go to work with Henri; however, Hurricane Katrina waylaid their plans.

A week after they arrived, the huge hurricane devastated the city Chris had come to love. He and his girlfriend fled the hurricane, but they had nowhere else to go. They drifted for a bit, but eventually, Chris heard from Henri, who was miraculously turning a tidy business despite the hurricane's destruction. Chris says, "The devastation was immense. It was like a third world country. There were piles of couches, refrigerators, everything ruined stacked in the middle of the street. Even McDonald's closed at 5:00 PM, and they could only serve very few items on the menu. Pretty much everything was closed, but not the tattoo shop. We absolutely could not believe that this shop could be so busy. We walked in, and immediately a guy wanted me to tattoo him. It was very crowded, and

use extra help during Mardi Gras. After walking around a while, I finally made it to Electric Expressions, which was a few blocks from the French Quarter. The artists working told me to come back later when the owner was there, so I left and went out to party for the night. I was wandering back to my hotel room, and I saw the 'Open' sign in the shop when I was passing by. I walked in, and I met Mr. Henri Montegut, who became one of my greatest mentors."

Henri checked out Chris's portfolio and offered to let him stay in his home to tattoo through the busy season. Chris worked for several weeks in New Orleans, and he loved the experience. Henri encouraged Chris to send some of his art to tattoo magazines and to start attending conventions, which helped mold the way he thought of the role of tattoo artists later in his career. After returning to Little Rock to work for a few more years, Chris

Some of Chris' favorite subject matter is from horror films.

The black background makes the blues even more striking.

Bella Lugosi's version of Dracula in purple.

An interesting composition.

there was a line of people waiting to get tattooed. Henri said that working at his shop during this time was like tattooing at Sturgis…it just didn't stop. It was so busy we didn't have time to do anything custom, just stuff off the wall, but I always altered the designs just a little. After doing this for a few months, I started buying up stuff to open my own shop."

Chris and his girlfriend, who pierced at Henri's shop, made all their money back, and after a few months, they moved to Arkansas and dove into opening Golden Lotus.

Golden Lotus has gained a national reputation and flowered into a successful enterprise, and Chris is proud of his accomplishments and the environment he has created for himself. He is grateful for Henri Montegut for bailing him out and allowing him the opportunity to work when so many people were suffering.

Chris' take on two versions of the Joker.

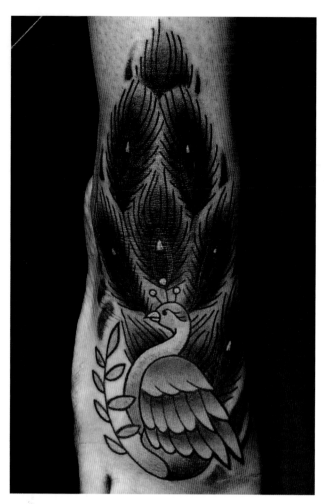

This Traditional peacock has heightened colors.

A Neo-Traditional chest panel.

At Golden Lotus, one way he has set himself apart from other shops in his area and in the industry generally is by attempting to make the entire process creative, from the design to the sale to his contact with his clients. He explains, "I try to make it all creative, every bit of it. Until the client and I meet eye to eye, the process won't work. It's really its own kind of creativity working with clients. It's its own art. You have to take that person's idea and make him or her happy with the way you put it together, putting that 'Wow' factor into the tattoo."

And Chris' clients love him for his charismatic "bedside" manner. Antoine, who is one of Chris' regular clients, explains, "Chris is a very funny guy, and he's really easy to talk to. There's always a funny situation or something coming up at the shop, and he's always right there in the middle of it. It's easy to get wrapped up in the comedy, and I'm constantly laughing when I'm there. At the same time, he's a very straightforward guy, and he will never bullshit you." Chris makes an effort to sell himself along with his art, which endears him to his clients and creates a self-propelling machine of promotion. "You have to be very outgoing in the tattoo business," says Chris, "or you will become stagnant. There are a lot of people in the industry who have been tattooing for decades that still have the same pitch, the same flash on the wall, and still tattoo the exact same way without ever wanting to experiment. It shows how creative they are with the client, too. You have really got to make your customer open his or her eyes, letting them know that ideas are endless. It's important to educate them about not just the tattoo aspect of it, but the artistic side of getting a good tattoo."

Golden Lotus is built with an open-floor to allow Chris to see the customers when they come in the door. It creates an exciting, noisy environment of controlled chaos, and it allows Chris the opportunity to talk a

A Nightmare sleeve by Chris Thomas.

Chris uses horror subjects to evoke a strong emotional response in the viewer.

Watercolor by Chris Thomas.

lot with clients and give feedback about all the tattoos that are being applied in his shop. "I sometimes wish I could be in my own, closed-off room when I'm deep into a project," he says, "but at the same time, I want to make sure all the right information is being given out to the customers who come in my shop. I deal with it, and I'm getting more and more used to talking, listening, and tattooing all at the same time."

IN HIS OWN WORDS: CHRIS THOMAS Q&A

Q: What do you remember about the first tattoo you ever did?

A: It was a cover-up of a small cross or something like that. We decided to put a burning Ace of Spades over the top of it. It was on my stepbrother, and it was about 4x6 inches. I decided to get a little tricky with it, just like every tattoo artist does at the beginning. I was trying to pull off color fades in the flames. I can honestly say it was not the worst tattoo I have ever seen, but it was by far not the best. Today, that little tattoo would take me maybe 45 minutes, but it took me 4 hours at the time I did it.

Digital painting by Chris Thomas.

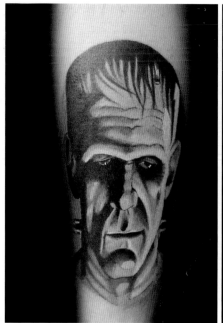

A pastel Frankenstein.

Terminator

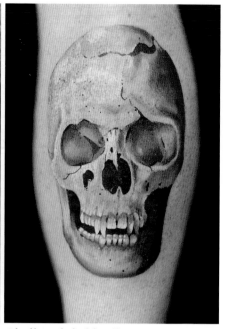

Skull with bold yellows.

I had no idea what I was doing. I know my machine was running very loud, but I had nobody to tell me what I was doing wrong or right or anything. At the time, I believed that if I were going to learn this trade, I'd have to do it on my own.

Q: What do you think about it today? Would you advise someone wanting to get into the industry to take the same approach?

A: You know, at the end of that tattoo, I was very happy with the outcome, and so was everybody else around me. After being so happy about this one, I decided it would be a great idea to put a tattoo on myself. I put a piece of tribal on my leg. Of course, it turned out really bad. I guess I was too excited and dumb all at the same time. I know a lot of people try to tattoo on themselves, but I will always say it is the worst idea, ever. I promise there are plenty of idiots in this

A leg sleeve with realistic faces.

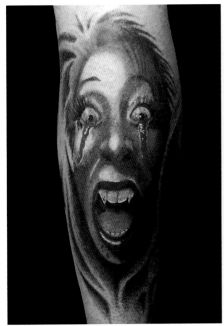

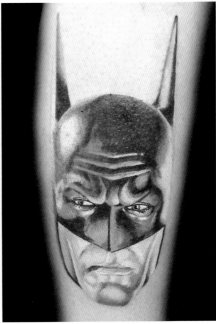

The placement on the leg enhances this face's shape.

Chris's interpretation of Batman.

Notice the painterly color blends in these blues.

world who would jump through hoops of fire to get a free tattoo. The bottom line is all the tattoos I did starting out sucked. If I had the chance to do it again, I would go about it in a totally different way. But what do you do? What's done is done, and I'm moving on to bigger and better things.

Q: What made you decide to pursue tattooing as your career?

A: I didn't get my first tattoo until I was 21. I traveled to Fresno, California, and while I was there, I saw a tattoo shop called Black Dragon. I got my first tattoo there, which was a cheesy small sun on my leg.

Like everybody says, tattoos are addictive, and I decided to get another one when I got back home to Shreveport. There was a shop in Shreveport then called Black Dragon also, but it wasn't related to the one in Fresno. A guy there named Scotty Allen tattooed

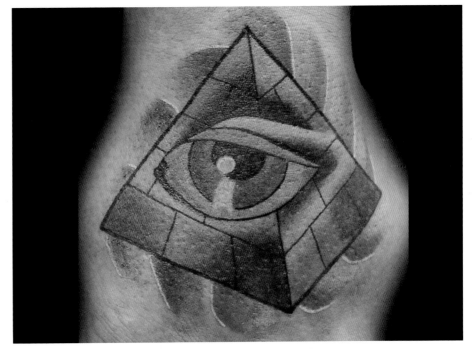

The hand is an interesting canvas for this tattoo.

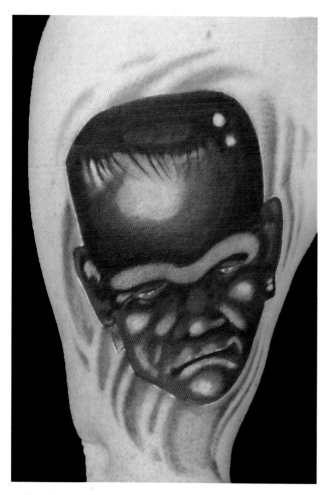

Chris has tattooed several versions of Frankenstein's monster.

and I went to work making some new drawings. I spent about a week making this sketchbook happen. I decided to get Scotty to do another tattoo, and I brought the sketchbook with me. After the tattoo was done, I handed him the book. It took him about 3 minutes to go through it. He handed it back to me and left it at that. He told me my drawings were good, but hell, for all I know he was just saying that so I would come get more ink from him. It was enough, though.

I decided to make it my goal to become a tattoo artist. Moving forward, I started making phone calls to different shops and trying to find out how to get my break.

Q: What kinds of tattoos do you think are the most meaningful?

A: I get a lot of memorial tattoos. The customers come in with the idea of a memorial for a

me the second time, and he was a real big influence on me wanting to start a career.

He did a lot of what we call freehand tattoos, where he would get a sharpie marker and just draw art on the skin and tattoo it. I thought it was pretty amazing that he could just look at a picture on the wall and immediately start drawing it on skin. When I was getting a tattoo from him one time, he asked me if I was an artist. I told him I was always good at making real cool drawings and paintings in school. My art teachers were always impressed with my work, and it was the one subject I actually enjoyed in school. Scotty asked me if I had some drawings I could bring and show him.

I got pretty excited, but when I looked at my art later, I realized most of them were pretty juvenile and didn't look like tattoo stuff. I went out and picked up a few tattoo magazines and a sketchbook,

A rare black and gray tattoo.

lost family member or close friend, and they want like the person's full name and birth and death dates. I usually go about it a little differently, asking them what was important to the lost loved ones and what they did in their lives that stands out so I could work something into the design. I usually try to talk them into something Traditional style, maybe with a banner that says something simple like "Mom" or "Dad" instead of a big line of words. It's better if it's something that symbolizes that person.

Q: Who are some of the tattoo artists that you admire?

A: I admire the art and tattoos of Chris Vennekamp and Brandon Bond. I would say I am heavily influenced by both of their styles. I also like the portrait style of Roman, who is at Artistic Element in California. Also, Darrin White from

Acrylic painting by Chris Thomas.

The swirling background colors provide contrast for the whites in the foreground.

North Carolina has been a big influence on my career. He has shown me how to do good black and gray and how to make images look exactly the way I need them to using Photoshop. It helps to get the picture to look exactly the way you want on the computer before you begin a tattoo, tweaking it and making it just right to suit the Chris Thomas taste and style.

Chapter Eight

John Wayne

Stings Like a Bee

"It hasn't been easy," says John Wayne of Belle River, Canada's Beesting Tattoo, "but I wouldn't trade it for anything in the world." This self-taught, self-employed, one-man-wonder has developed a distinct style and a technical mastery through years of doing it the wrong way. While he does not recommend that others follow in his footsteps, his unusual path to success in the tattoo industry has crossed with many of the art's legends, and John's unique ability to learn by watching and doing have helped him to leave his own lasting impact.

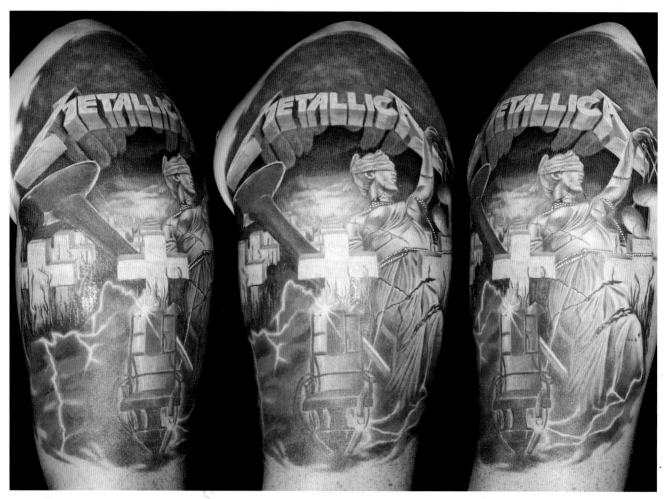

Metallica tribute.

His Background

"My first tattoo?" says John when asked about the memory. He hesitates to answer, but smiles and says, "I was skipping out of school. It was 1989, and I had a sewing needle and some ink for a fountain pen. I drew a little cross on my wrist. I guess you could say it started there." His next step was to build his own tattoo machine from scratch, which he says, "was a huge mistake! I had to fix all those tattoos later as I got better. It took a lot of time figuring out how to handle all those cover-ups."

John picked up his first professional tattoo machine in 1995, which is where he cites the beginning of his real career as a tattooist. Prior to that year, he had been working as an airbrush artist and was doing freelance illustration. He would tattoo a few folks here and there, whom friends would bring to him. He says, "When friends would drop by with somebody looking for a tattoo, I just could not turn anyone away. I

John Wayne is known as a master of detail.

loved the artwork of tattooing, but I wasn't confident that I could pull that kind of art off on skin." Eventually, however, he realized that his heart was not in the other work he was doing, and he began to seek out ways to learn more about tattooing.

Once John decided to pursue tattooing more seriously, he had begun to get tattoos at a local shop, and he had been seeking guidance from some of the artists. He explains, "After five years of tattooing on my own, I felt like it was just going nowhere. I needed some help to start moving in another direction. Two artists at the local shop, Aron Mackenzie and Darren Trudell, showed me some basic techniques to help me start doing a little better."

After a few months of practicing with these new techniques, John teamed up with Aron and moved to another local shop. They spent a few more months swapping techniques with each other and anyone else who would share their experience. John says, "For a few years, I did a lot of pretty straightforward flash tattooing, and I bought a lot of tattoo magazines to see what other people were doing. I tried to copy some of the techniques I saw there."

John and Jackie Wayne are partners in Beesting Tattoo.

One of John's favorite tattoos is the geisha he put on Jackie's arm.

This bloody vampire girl is one of John's favorite pieces.

A classic portrait of Johnny Cash.

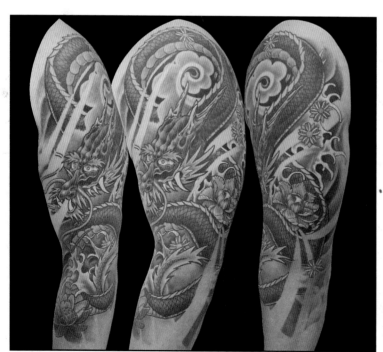

Notice the details in the scales.

Eventually, however, John felt he had reached another plateau, and he sought out new ways to grow his arsenal of tattoo techniques. He had heard good things about Deano Cook's Color Realism seminar, and in 2005, he signed up at the Detroit Convention. He cites this experience as transforming his technical ability, and he began looking for more opportunities to interact with established artists so that he could learn their skills. "Between Deano Cook's seminar and getting tattooed by Bob Tyrell and Larry Brogan, I learned a lot," says John. "Both Bob and Larry have helped me out greatly in perfecting my techniques. I am sure I would not have figured this stuff out for a long time."

While it is not the traditional route of apprenticeship, John's scavenging of tattoo technique has served him well, and he has had good instincts about when it is appropriate to seek outside influences. "When you seem to be following a path that feels comfortable, it's hard to change," he explains, "It has worked really well for me to find

Black and gray portraits frequently commemorate lost relatives.

John's black and gray portraiture is highly realistic.

John achieves realistic depth in the facial wrinkles.

a style of artist I identify with and to get tattooed by him or her and to study the techniques. If that artist is really cool, like Larry or Bob, then he or she will be more than willing to answer any of your questions, as long as you don't get annoying."

From these experiences, John has established a personal cure for himself when he feels that his art reaches a plateau. When he reaches a stagnant place, he says, "It's at that moment that I decide to take some seminars or go and get a lot of ink from other artists. I basically start studying new styles and looking past the kind of work that I normally do. I try to look beyond where I usually look and appreciate different styles. Even if I won't do a tattoo in that style, I can appreciate it for a technique or for the way it flows with the body." This open-minded, open-ended approach to his artistic education has lead to a diverse portfolio with notable leaps in skill after he conquers each new creative battle.

Beautiful realism is evident in these portraits; notice the contouring in the cheeks.

107

John's version of the Phoenix from Marvel comics.

A classic motorcycle theme.

This joker seems to be lit from behind.

HIS STYLE

"I really don't feel like I tattoo anything so unique like say Aaron Cain or Guy Aitchison," says John of his artistic style. While his compositions might not be as radical as some other artists, many elements of a John Wayne tattoo make them recognizable, particularly his commitment to detail in his realistic pieces.

"I think my color work is strong," he says, "and I try to apply a lot of depth to achieve it. I also like to pay real close attention to the details. My clients would tell you that they love and hate the details I put in!" Despite the pain required for the wearer, the details make a John Wayne tattoo truly special. In his dog portrait (page 105), for

Startling realism in John's interpretation of the Joker.

instance, the realistic textures in the hair and the white lines that create an impression of wetness

108

around the dog's eyes and nose heighten the realism significantly.

Unlike many color realists, John also is adept at black and gray tattooing. His attention to detail translates well from color realism. In his version of Johnny Cash (page 106), for instance, he translates the textures in his skin, shirt, hair, guitar strap, and more. The distinctions between each element of the portrait, such as the realistic folds in the shirt and the illusion of light glinting off the guitar strings, make this piece truly memorable.

John also frequently applies his attention to detail and penchant for bold colors to Asian style artwork. In his koi fish (page 110), which is a common enough subject for tattoos, he adds a clean, crisp composition and realistic sheen in the eye to make it unique. Similarly, he re-invigorates the Asian dragon (page 106) in his composition. He takes the traditional wind bars, cherry blossoms, and whiskered, horned dragon tattoo and tightens it up with clean lines, three-dimensional perspective, tiny details, and stark contrast in the colors. Here he combines a respect for the ancient Japanese tradition in his subject matter and composition, but he adds new life and his own signature style.

In addition to Bob Tyrell and Larry Brogan, whose tattoo techniques influenced John enough that he sought them out to do his own work, he includes artist Aaron Cain as one of his greatest influences. "I saw his work in 1991 in a tattoo magazine," he says, "and I was blown away. It was amazing to me that this guy could tattoo better than most people I had seen draw on paper. He is still tops in my book, both for his application of the tattoos and for his imaginative creativity in his compositions." He cites Jack Rudy as well for being influential early in his career, and recently, he admires Guy Aitchison, Marshall Bennett, Mike Devries, Nikko Hurtato, Don MacDonald, Nate Beavers, Josh Woods, Joe Capobianco, and Robert Hernandez. His list of influences is diverse, but overall, he reveals these artists as sources of his strong attraction to the photorealistic trend that has emerged in tattooing.

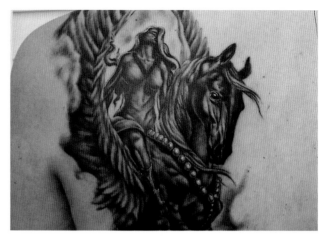

John's careful placement of this tattoo on the shoulder blade enhances the wearer's natural anatomy.

A chest plate with Traditional American influence.

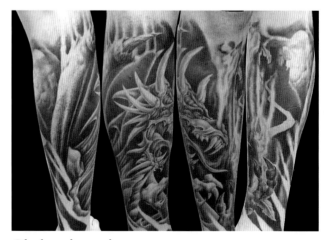

Black and gray dragon.

Bettie Page as a mummy.

HIS BUSINESS

After scavenging for many years to acquire a level of technical expertise with which he is satisfied, John now runs a one-man tattoo shop out of his home in Belle River, Canada. His wife Jackie is his business partner, and he enjoys having the opportunity to share his passion for tattooing with her, mixing business and pleasure. He explains, "I have a great family life. My wife and I are lucky to be able to work together every day. She is always there to encourage me when I seem to come up against a wall creatively. I don't see myself the way she and the rest of my family see me."

He calls his shop Beesting Tattoo, and he and his wife have carefully refined their business processes to maximize everyone's experience. When a client arrives at Beesting, he or she first sits down with Jackie, who makes an appointment, discusses the money, and takes careful notes about the project. Next, the client will sit with John to design the tattoo. By including the client in his

creative process, John saves time. He rarely has to re-draw a design, as the client pre-approves his sketches before the day of the tattoo. The final step is the application of the tattoo itself. The division of labor between the creative side for John and the business side for his wife suits both perfectly, and he appreciates Jackie's commitment to growing their family business through her business savvy.

John admits, however, that the business end is still a lot of work, even with his wife holding the reigns, and at times, it can interfere with his creativity. He says, "The business end requires a lot from both of us, which is something the client does not see too often. It's not the glamour they see on television. The amount of preparation it takes to get to the actual inking sometimes takes longer than applying the tattoo itself."

A koi fish with John's characteristic bold colors

John and his wife spread the word about Beesting, which is important for an artist living in a small town. He says, "We promote ourselves through magazines and online tattoo forums, my own website, t-shirts, conventions, stickers, business cards, really everything." Belle River is only 20 miles from Detroit, so they have access to the advantages of a major city; however, without spreading the word about the quality of art John is capable of producing, it is less likely that a client would cross the border to get a tattoo.

While Belle River is small, John says that his clientele is devoted to the acquisition of the indelible art. "It's crazy!" he says. "People will miss their anniversaries, surgeries, and just about any day of work just to get in for a tattoo it seems. Over the years, the tattoos have gotten a lot bigger around here as well. What used to be considered a big tattoo is starting to be considered medium or small."

Bettie Page Frankenstein.

The tweaked perspective on this frog makes it unique.

IN HIS OWN WORDS:
JOHN WAYNE Q&A

Q: What's your favorite tattoo that you've done?

A: I would have to say that my most favorite piece that I have done to date is the geisha tattoo (page 106) that I put on my wife's arm. I also really like the bloody vampire girl face (page 106). It is my second favorite.

Q: Do you identify with a style of tattooing, or is one your favorite?

A: Lately, I am finding myself really drawn to the biomechanical or organic style. I also like the painted portrait style of tattooing. I like tattoos that look airbrushed more than tattooed.

Q: What do you think of the changes in the tattoo industry since you first got started as a professional?

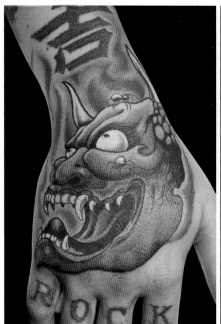

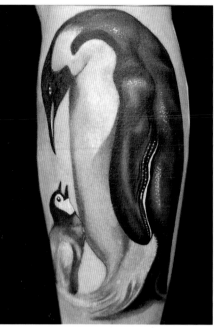

Note the interesting placement and perspective for this Japanese mask.

Penguin mother and child.

John combines several tattoo styles in this clever composition.

Two koi fish with a lotus.

A: I think the creativity in the industry today is by far the best it has ever been. In such a short period of time, tattooing has gone from a "pick it and stick it" way of thinking to something that has so much better flow. People now think about how the tattoo will compliment the body, and that's new for a lot of us. They've always done it in Asian and Polynesian style tattooing, but not in a lot of other styles. I feel that there really are no more boundaries, nothing at all, to stop us from doing whatever we want in tattooing. More and more, newer artists are getting into tattooing, and we are starting to see what could only be done as illustrations on paper or canvas appearing on skin. I believe that we are currently in a Renaissance of art, and I truly believe in years to come, people will look back on this time in tattooing as a great movement. I think we'll read about tattoo artists like we read about Michelangelo or Leonardo da Vinci and how they changed painting. I'm not so much comparing any of today's artists, but the changes we're making…the movement itself.

Q: *How would you describe those changes?*

A: I feel the industry is becoming more business-like…more professional…and more family friendly. Parents will take their kids to get their first tattoos, or older people that were afraid to get one when they were younger, afraid of what others would have to say about them, are coming in and getting tattoos now. The industry is becoming populated with all walks of life. All kinds of people want to be part of something so expressive to the world with no regrets. The quality of the art, also, and the quality in the safety, sanitation and cleanliness, have been a big part of the massive explosion in this industry in my opinion.

Q: *I know that going to conventions has played a big role in your development as an artist. Now that you're a business owner, how often are you able to get to shows?*

A: I try to attend three shows per year: Detroit, Toronto, and Halifax. Traveling to these shows requires a lot more work than some people might think. It's a lot of work just to get to the event, packing up all the equipment and everything, and once you are there, it's just go! Go! GO! The nice part, though, is that you have a chance to leave your mark on a different part of the world, and you get to see artists doing their work. I would love to travel a bit further down into the States, possibly checking out a show in Los Angeles or even southern, like down toward Texas.

Q: *What's your favorite show?*

A: So far, my favorite is definitely Detroit. It's close to home, which cuts down on some of the hassle, and it always brings out some huge name artists.

Q: *Tell us about Belle River.*

A: It's in Ontario, Canada, and it's where I grew up for most of my life. My parents moved my two brothers and me here when we were really small, and I've been around ever since. Belle River is a very small town. Right now, we have about 10,000 people, but when I was growing up, there

Cars offer John a unique opportunity to employ his technical mastery.

John makes the tribal butterfly much more interesting with a more detailed composition.

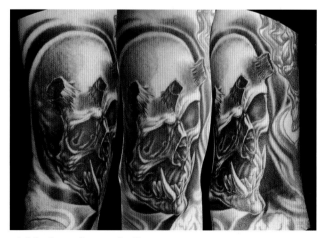

A black and gray skull

Realistic shading in this Spiderman gives it superb three-dimensionality.

A: My social life has definitely changed since we've been in business. It's hard to socialize just as a person rather than as a tattoo artist. People seem to think that you are always working even when all you want to do is relax and enjoy a day off.

Q: *How do you think you've evolved through the years as an artist? Have you gone through a lot of phases, or is your art pretty much the same?*

A: Oh, yeah, I've gone through phases. My tattooing has evolved or transformed a few times. At first, it really was just about trying to keep the ink in the skin. I did not use a lot of imagination. It was more like basic coloring, almost like filling in a coloring book for kids. Then, as I tried some other new techniques, my work started to look like the flash on the walls. It wasn't the most creative stuff, but it got stronger technically. So far, the latest stage in my tattooing has turned to the painted style. Right now, it's portraits and color realism most of the time.

was something like 3,000 or 4,000. It is really just your typical small community, where everyone knows everyone and everybody helps each other out. We are only 20 minutes from Detroit, so it's nice to be able to be close to a big city. Belle River has shaped me into being an artist without the rock star attitude. I still have a small town complex, so when I get near big-name artists, I still get star struck. These folks are the idols in my industry!

Q: *What do you do when you aren't tattooing? Do you have many hobbies?*

A: I love to cruise on my beach cruiser bicycle, and I collect tattoo machines. I'm really an Internet junkie, so I spend a lot of my down time online. Also, I recently have been trying my hand at painting again. It is good to get back on canvas. It gives me some new perspective on what it is that I would create for myself for a change instead of doing what I'm asked to do for others.

Q: *What's your social life like?*

The realism in the hand and the translucence of the skin are impressive in this piece.

Q: *What do you remember about the first tattoo you ever put on?*

A: Well, I did one on myself with a needle and some ink. It was a little cross on my wrist. My first actual, real tattoo on a real client in a shop was a little flower on a girl's ankle. I was terrified to do it. It was scary to tattoo somebody I didn't know, and if I screwed up, I knew I'd be done early in the industry for sure. It went fine, though, and she loved it.

Q: *Do you have a memorable client or a funny story about somebody?*

A: Well, one client in particular stands out more than anyone else. I am sure there are other artists who can relate to this story! There was this guy who blacked out while I was tattooing him for about two minutes, and while he was passed out, he pissed his pants. I felt really bad for him, but he assured me that it happens to him a lot!

Q: *How do you see yourself changing as an artist?*

A: I would like to become more of a specialty artist, you know? Like how Bob Tyrell is with black and gray. I also want to turn more to the biomechanical style or organic art, and maybe mix it up with a little industrial.

Q: *If you had some advice to give to a new artist, what would it be?*

A: I would have to say that just attending the conventions and speaking with other artists helped me more than anything else. I asked a lot of questions and a lot of people were really helpful when I was trying to learn. It almost feels like we are all really connected in this industry. Everybody seems to have a similar story or two. The deeper I go into the tattooing world, the more people I meet, the more things seem to change about the way I tackle new pieces. It's all helping me to grow as an artist.

A black and gray sleeve.

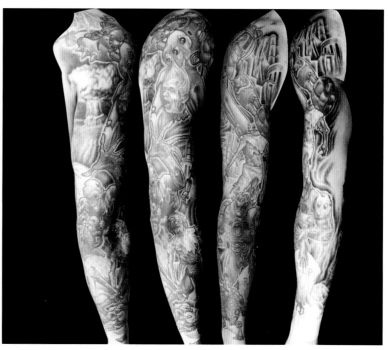

A zombie sleeve in black and gray with red highlights

115

Chapter Nine

Amanda Wachob

The Fine Art of Tattoo

"Painting and tattooing have formed a symbiotic relationship in my life," says Amanda Wachob of her two artistic passions. Amanda is emblematic of a new movement in the tattoo world, bringing her background in fine art and applying it to the human canvas.

The resulting body of work is a refreshing juxtaposition of fine art principles with tattoo sensibility.

HER BACKGROUND

"I went to Purchase College in Westchester, New York," says Amanda of her

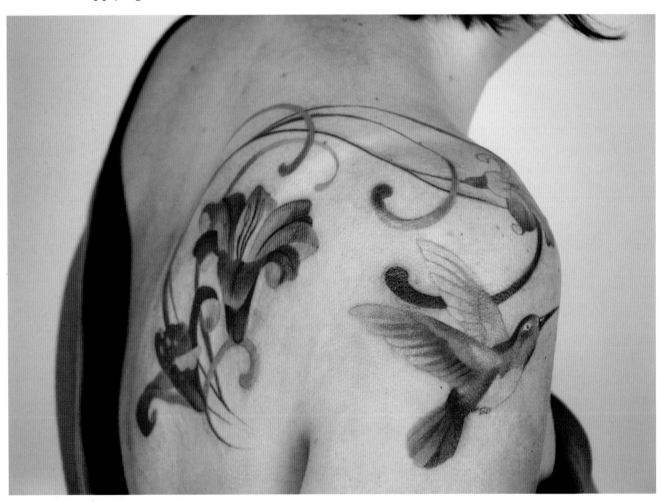

Hummingbird with flowers.

education. "I always had a lot of friends who dabbled with tattooing in the college dorms. I thought it was fascinating." Like many young artists, she graduated with a fine arts degree and found herself largely unemployable. She relocated to a small town in the Hudson Valley region of New York State, and struggled to find work using her photography skills. She explains, "All I knew was that I did not want to be a commercial photographer. I was also frustrated by the fact that I didn't have access to a darkroom, so it was going to be hard for me to continue to print my photographs. A good friend of mine at the time was an illustrator and a tattoo artist. He encouraged me to pursue tattooing, and he said that it was a great way for an artist to earn an income and still be able to make art. I brought some of my

While Amanda frequently tattoos abstract compositions, she is also adept with more traditional styles.

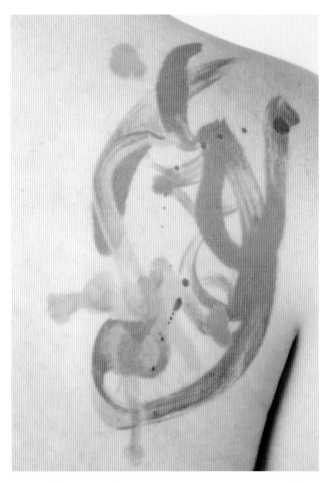

Amanda views Abstract Expressionism as a new frontier in tattooing.

drawings into a local shop to show the owners, and I landed an apprenticeship." It was august of 1998 when she began her career as a tattooist, and in the intervening decade, she has continued to find ways to expand what it is possible to achieve in a tattoo.

HER STYLE

Amanda's portfolio is one of the most diverse in the tattoo world. While she is able to apply her virtuosic skill to a technically difficult tattoo, such as a large-scale Japanese backpiece, much of her more recent work emerges from the Abstract Expressionist movement in painting. Instead of recreating an image on the wearer, many of Amanda's pieces serve as adornments, changing the wearer him or herself into the subject matter of the tattoo. The tattoo art itself becomes secondary;

Amanda captures the essence of a flock of birds …

Other art movements that have influenced Amanda's unique approach to tattooing include Kirlian photography and Aura photography. In her art education, she had focused on art photography, and she found the mystic, metaphysical aspects of these photographic movements to be intriguing. She says, "Both types of photography have been used to document the colors and energy fields around living organisms. They show that every human being emits something unique, much like a fingerprint."

Tattoo art has long been associated with personal expression and an individual's desire to mark him or herself as unique, and Amanda's abstract work takes the idea of a custom tattoo to a new level. Not only will a wearer have a tattoo that has been custom-designed for him or her, but these works are

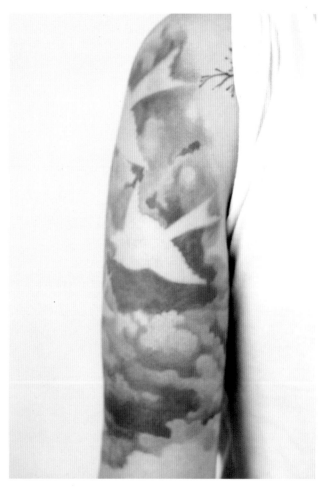

…moving across the sky without black lines.

instead, the emphasis is on the person who has been tattooed.

"I've always been fascinated by color," says Amanda. "I have always loved doing odd, quirky art-oriented tattoos. The abstract work I do now evolved from this theme in my work." When she began tattooing, she studied the various trends and styles of tattoo art, and she began comparing them to the various movements in painting. She explains, "I was looking at Abstract Expressionists like Helen Frankenthaler and Hans Hoffman wondering why no one had thought to approach tattooing in this sense—to move away from the representational image. Why couldn't tattoos just be about form and color? Instead of focusing on a representation of something, color can say so much about a person."

118

also unique in that they do not look like other tattoos. They do not look like each other, even. There is a stylistic similarity, as Amanda's color palette and distinctive linework are recognizable in each tattoo; however, these tattoos truly evoke a one-of-a-kind relationship between the wearer, the viewer, and the artist.

Like aural photography or the uncanny electrical images that appear in a Kirlian photograph, Amanda's abstractions allow each of us to interpret the swirling colors, the lines and places where they trail off or dissolve into the wearer's natural physiognomy, according to our own emotional responses. There is no history, no theme, nor weighty tradition underlying these designs as there are in a more figurative style.

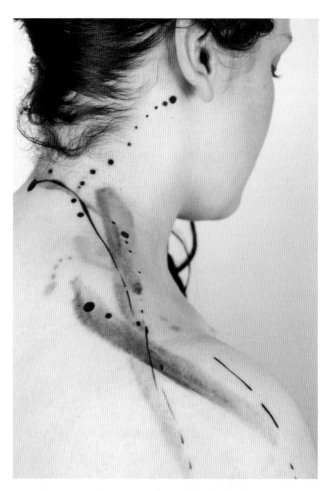

In this piece, the wearer herself is the subject matter; the tattoo's presence is secondary to her own.

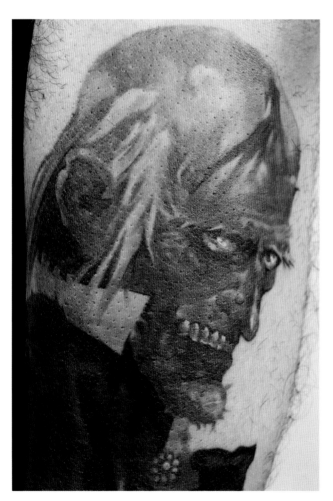

This portrait is done without black lines

In New York City, where Amanda is working today, there is a strong strain of Traditional American tattooing. Amanda's abstract work stands out starkly against this strong tradition. She explains, "New York is really surprisingly very conservative. Most artists here are working in the Traditional style these days. Don't get me wrong…I love vintage flash. I love Owen Jensen and Sailor Jerry, but I get the sense that people are craving something different in their tattoos. Tattooing is supposed to be about self-expression. So I often wonder why so many of the tattoo artists here pat themselves on the back for making everyone look the same."

Other aspects that make Amanda's work stand out in the tattoo industry are her unique

119

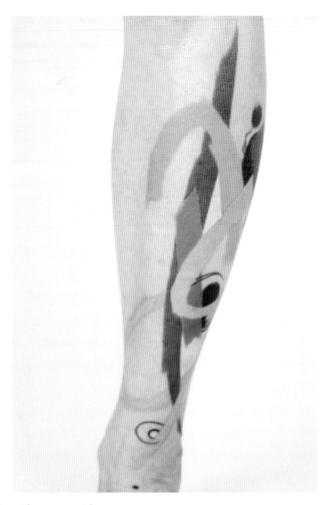

Abstract work...

color palette and her aversion to the black outline. While tattoo artists have been transgressing the "Bold Will Hold" mentality that marked the lining philosophy of Traditional American style tattoo art for a few decades, Amanda's resistance to the figurative constraints of tattoo linework is particularly notable. In her negative-space bird half-sleeve, for instance, she creates the illusion of a flock of birds moving across a field of sky, all without the use of hard, black outlines. Also, in her portrait of a creepy old man, she adds a unique spin on the photorealistic trend that has taken over the tattoo world in the last decade, rendering the image with painterly, muted colors and few hard lines. The juxtaposition of the softness of her colorwork with the man's sinister expression creates a disconcerting effect in the viewer.

AMANDA TODAY

After working for a few years as part-owner of Blue Moon in Buffalo, New York, which is her hometown, Amanda has returned to New York City. She opened Blue Moon in 2003, and while she loves Buffalo, she had missed New York and its arts scene. She says, "I'm from Buffalo, which is the second largest city in New York State, second in line to New York City. It is a poor city with a struggling economy. Buffalo is the ultimate underdog. I identify with the underdog. Now, I live and work in New York City. I recently joined the team at Dare Devil Tattoo, which is owned by Michelle Myles and Brad Fink. I love working on the Lower East Side. There is a very raw

... by Amanda Wachob

Amanda's take on …

… Traditional American subject matter.

Sugar skulls with flowers.

A sleeve.

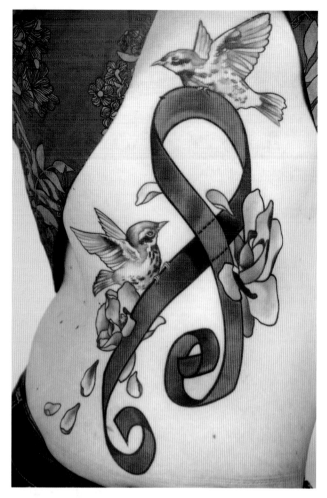

The sketchy, loose feel of this tattoo creates a light, feminine piece.

energy down here." Dare Devil Tattoo is one of the two oldest tattoo shops in New York City.

While her radical approach to tattooing has drawn much attention to Amanda as a tattoo artist, she is also well known in the fine arts world. Where tattooing is public, collaborative, and interactive, Amanda views painting as being her private expression of her creative ideas and impulses. She explains, "Working with a client on a custom piece can be challenging. Trying to adhere to the customer's idea while maintaining artistic integrity…Painting is just for me, when I need to be solitary and please nobody but myself."

Amanda has shown her paintings in several exhibitions, including solo shows in Arizona, Virginia, and New York.

IN HER OWN WORDS: AMANDA WACHOB Q&A

Q: Tell us about your early career.
A: I had a rough apprenticeship. I wasn't treated very nicely, and those first few years were a real struggle. I'm sure many of us in the industry had similar experiences and could say the same thing. But really, I'm glad it was not too easy for me. It made me want to work harder and really to push myself to excel at tattooing. I'm grateful for that difficult time.

The sunset color palette in this tattoo is unique.

122

Notice the realistic details in this fish.

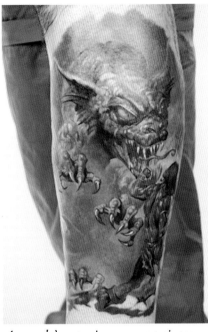

Amanda's experience as a painter serves her well in the painterly touches she adds to these pieces.

A sleeve with mythic themes.

Q: *What do you remember about your first tattoo?*

A: It was on a close friend who, despite my protests, insisted on having the very first tattoo I ever did. The tattoo was of the Peanuts character Linus holding his blanket. The whole design was only about three inches in size, but it must have taken me six hours to execute. I was so nervous, and my hands were shaking. I kept having to stop and take breaks. I guess it was good, though, that I went slowly because thankfully, the tattoo still looks pretty decent.

Q: *Who are some of the tattoo artists you admire?*

A: Cynthia Witkin, Jon Clue, Guy Aitchison, Vyvyn Lazonga, and Grime were big influences on me when I first started. I also really love how ahead of his time George Burchett was. He developed cosmetic tattooing back in the 1930's. And I like that he helped to elevate tattooing out of some of its

Poppies

While Amanda tends to avoid figurative pieces, this portrait showcases her technical skill.

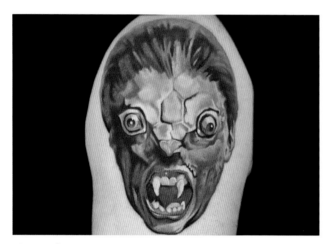

A reptilian creature.

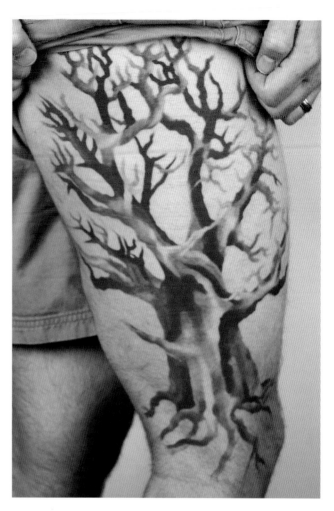

Black and gray tree

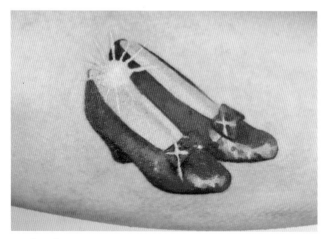

Ruby Slippers.

negative class associations by regularly inking the European royalty. These days, I think Nick Baxter is pretty innovative, and Josh Lord puts a lot of care and attention to detail in his work. And, I owe a lot to Jason D'Aquino. Over the years, he has been a huge inspiration to me, both in his tattooing and his art.

Q: Is there a particular style with which you identify?

A: I love doing the abstract pieces. I am so completely absorbed in the process, from making the initial painting to the application of the tattoo.

Q: Is there a client or a tattoo that is particularly memorable?

A: I once did a giant five-inch pair of smoochy red lips on the derriere of a 76-year-

This abstract piece recalls Japanese calligraphy.

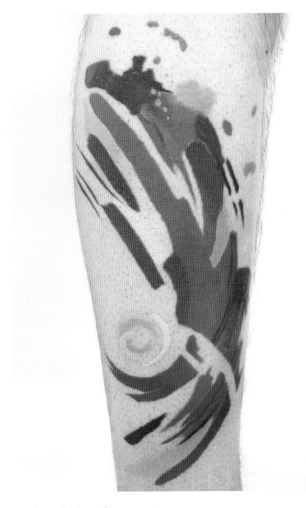

Red and blue abstract piece.

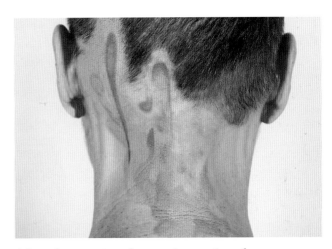

This abstract piece features interesting placement.

old man. It was his first tattoo. I giggled the entire time.

Q: *How do you promote your work?*

A: When the customer leaves the shop and shows off his or her art to other people, and when clients talk about the experience they had getting tattooed—word of mouth is the best form of promotion. It has also helped me to be heavily involved in another form of art. Painting and tattooing feed each other, even in terms of press and other publicity.

Q: *What do you do when you're not tattooing?*

A: When I'm not working, I'm painting. Or, I'm on the hunt for the Flying Spaghetti Monster. I also like pool, single malt scotch, chocolate cigarettes, and 130 mile-per-hour 1968 Triumph Bonneville rides. I wish I had

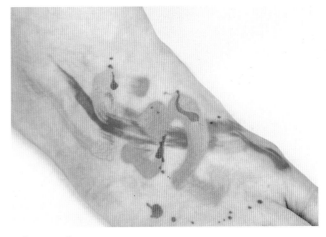

Abstract foot piece.

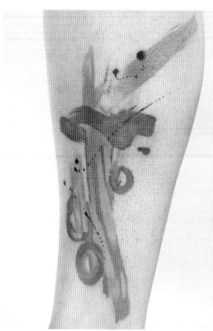 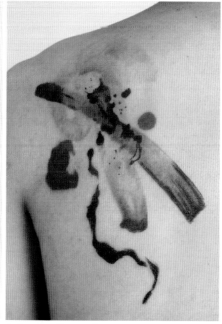 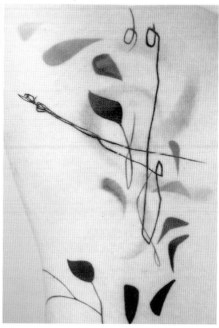

Pink and gold abstract piece

The small touches of color add interest to this piece.

Abstract in black and gray

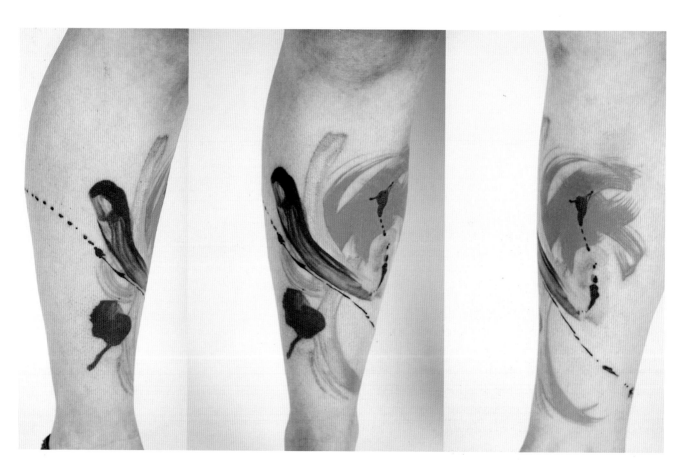

Abstract piece by Amanda Wachob

more time to spend with my family and friends. Art monopolizes so much of my time that my social life and relationships suffer a little. It is hard to find a balance.

Q: Do you see your work changing?

A: I am always thinking of how to evolve, how to look at tattooing differently. From a technical standpoint, I am working on becoming faster.

Q: What do you do when you find yourself getting stuck? Do you ever feel like you are in a rut artistically?

A: Usually, when complacency sets in, it means a big change is in order for me. In this case, it was selling the shop that I had owned for five years in Buffalo. I think it is so important to leave your comfort zone and try some-

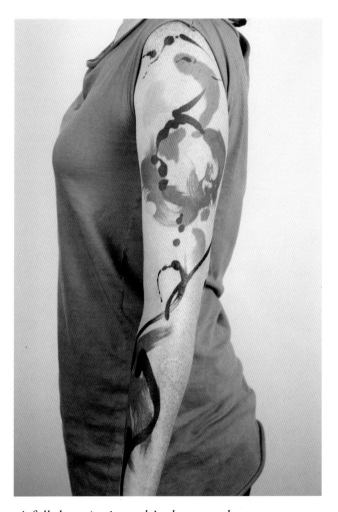

A full sleeve in Amanda's abstract style

In her paintings, Amanda often uses images reminiscent of the 1950s.

thing new whenever you have reached a plateau in your life. Change is a good way to check to make sure that you still have a pulse, personally and artistically.

Chapter Ten

Joshua Carlton

Ghostley Realism

"You can't tattoo that way, kid. It won't last." Tattoo industry old-timers hounded Joshua Carlton when he dropped the thick, black outlines he'd been trained to include in every tattoo. The "bold will hold" theory has dominated tattoo art, particularly in the Traditional American and Asian styles, for decades. The idea is that, although all tattoos will fade with time, the thick, black outlines common in most Traditional style tattoos would allow the image to be recognizable many years later.

Joshua Carlton admits that he could never be a Traditionalist.

Early in his career, Joshua dropped the outlines and picked up a 15-magnum needle. He explains, "I try to keep in mind that these guys must know what they are talking about. Otherwise, they would not have been around for so long. But I started questioning what it was that made a tattoo hold up. Was it really the outline? I doubted it, seeing the blurry outlines on old men in the grocery store. It turns out that a strong foundation is what is needed to make a tattoo last."

These realizations lead Joshua to develop one of the most recognizable styles in the tattoo world today. His soft, painterly approach and delicate chiaroscuro have gained him a reputation as one of the finest artists in the United States, particularly in the emerging realist movement.

His Background

Although Joshua was born in Prescott, Arizona, he does not have much of a memory of the place. "We moved several times throughout my childhood," he says. "My father was always looking for a better life for us. I was able to spend my entire high school years in Corvallis, Oregon, so I definitely have strong memories there, which is probably where the outdoorsy side of me comes from."

The beautiful natural scenery was an early inspiration for Joshua. He says, "Oregon is such a beautiful place. It is easy to be creative when such beautiful nature is everywhere you look. In the winter, it rains about every other day, which can be depressing for some people, but I found that those rainy days made good inspiration for me to draw all day long."

Joshua did not set out to become a tattoo artist, but from childhood he was inclined to the arts. As a child, he had his heart set on being a photographer. He explains, "It was all I wanted to do, and you would never see me without my camera. One day, though, my older sister got a tattoo, and she started dating a tattoo artist. Suddenly, this new art form became very appealing to me. I talked her boyfriend into letting me use his equipment one night,

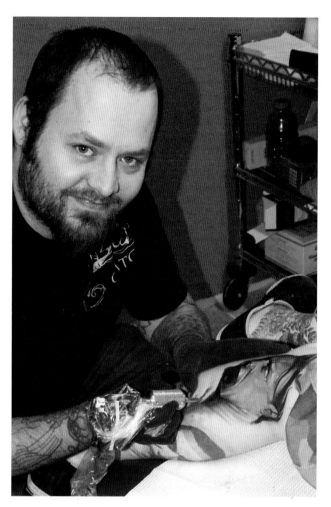

Joshua Carlton working.

and I tattooed myself. As crude as the artwork was, I was immediately hooked. Photography quickly became a distant memory. I hear this all the time from other artists, but I truly feel like tattooing came calling to me."

Tattoo artists are frequently rule-breakers, and while most who have acquired their skills through self-teaching would not advise new tattooists to do the same, many of the industry's best began their careers in their kitchens and bathrooms. Joshua says, "I am self-taught. There wasn't one tattoo shop in the town I grew up in. The closest one was in Portland, which was about an hour away." While he was in high school, Joshua didn't have the means to make it to the Portland shop, so he dove in headfirst.

129

Blood red lips and roses make this piece memorable.

.

He says, "I bought books and magazines, devouring anything with the word 'tattoo' on it. I built up a strong portfolio, knowing I would have to prove my abilities to be able to get accepted into a reputable shop."

After several months of working on himself and friends brave enough to allow the burgeoning artist to experiment, Joshua met Steve Hayworth, who is best known for his extreme body modifications. "Steve was in the process of building a new shop that offered custom tattooing," says Joshua. "I convinced him that I was his guy, and he gave me my first professional shot."

HIS STYLE

While color realism and painterly portraiture have become increasingly popular in recent years, Joshua has long been a proponent of this style of tattooing. From figures taken straight out of classic horror movies to other less-common sources of inspiration, Joshua seeks out source material that will create a disconcerting tension in the viewer. His soft palette, delicate shading, and crisp chiaroscuro render each image undeniably beautiful; however, the discomfort arises from the psychologically disturbing subject matter.

In his portrait of a woman with roses bursting from her eyes, for instance, Joshua creates this sense of tension. The red, wet-seeming lips and the smooth, realistic skin in the woman's face are beautiful. The petals of the roses appear brilliant red, highlighting her lips, and the textures seem supple and silky. The viewer

A color interpretation of Bella Lugosi's classic vampire.

wants to appreciate the beauty of these two elements separately, but they are undeniably, distressingly linked, requiring us to imagine how the roses came to be placed in her eye sockets. The combination of gorgeous and gruesome marks the best of Joshua's work.

Joshua considers a strong, dark background to be as effective in helping a tattoo withstand the test of time as the bold outlines most commonly used by his Traditional American predecessors. Through his years of tattooing, he has come to associate his process of putting an image together with that of Rembrandt. He explains, "I've always been a huge fan of Rembrandt, as well as other old master painters who put a heavy emphasis on strong shadows. I started using them as my influence and refer-

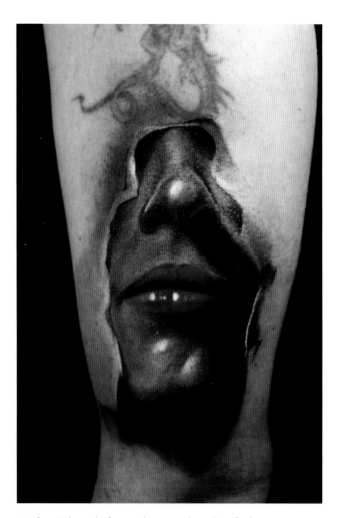

Joshua's knack for realism makes this flesh tear impressive.

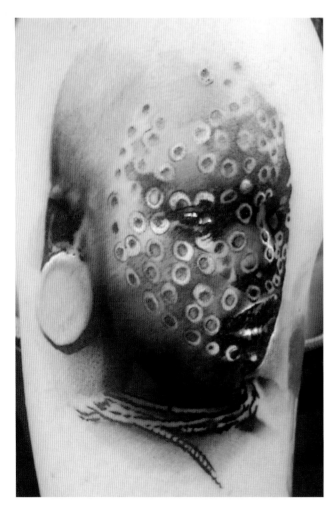

A portrait celebrating the roots of body modification.

ence, kind of setting out to prove that realism can be achieved in tattooing without some of the old standards. I try to take a more painterly approach.

Over the last five years or so, the color realism movement that has rocked the tattoo world has inspired Joshua. While Joshua has always focused on realism in his work, he concentrated largely on black and gray portraiture. He says, "Even though I have always done realism, it just seemed natural to do it in black and gray since that was all that everyone who came before me did. I never even gave it much thought to do color in my portraits. I was afraid that it would take on the look of a cartoon. I started seeing some amazing color realism popping up in the magazines and on the

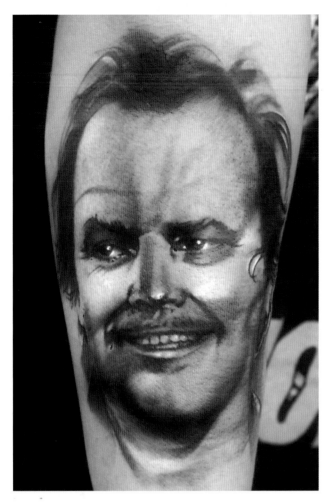

Joshua is known for using color highlights in black and gray portraiture.

I've always been a little bit of a computer geek. I tattoo full-time still, so I'm constantly adding to my portfolio on and offline, and I always try to send work in to the tattoo magazines. This exposure has given me a strong, loyal clientele, and kept me happily tattooing through the years."

Shelbyville, Indiana, is about 45 minutes south of Indianapolis. In 2000, Joshua packed up his life in Arizona, where he was living at the time, and moved to Indiana to work with the artist Monte Agee in the capital city. Monte is well known throughout the industry for breathtaking, large-scale, realistic pieces. While working in Indy, he met his wife Nicole, who was originally from Shelbyville. He traveled with her to visit her family from time to time,

A tribute to Kurt Cobain.

Internet, and this gave me a spark similar to when I first started. It set me on the second path of my career in tattooing. Color has now encapsulated my work so much that if you are newly discovering me as an artist, you may not realized that I have a black and gray past."

HIS BUSINESS

Joshua never considered himself to be much of a businessman, putting the emphasis in his career on his development as an artist. However, as do many artists, he eventually tired of working for other people and decided to go out on his own. He says, "It wasn't until I opened my own shop, The Great American Tattoo Co, in Shelbyville, Indiana, that I opened my mind to the business side of things. I started to maintain a heavy web presence, as

132

and Joshua liked the small-town feel. Because there wasn't a tattoo shop in town, he thought it would be a great place to settle, start a business, and begin raising his family.

Joshua is now the proud father of two children. Despite the pressures of being a tattoo artist, which requires long hours, travel, and lots of off time devoted to designing and researching new pieces, he says, "My family is extremely supportive of my career, especially my wife. She has been there with me through it all. Balancing work and family leaves me little time for a social life, but I choose to keep it that way. I would rather focus my free time on painting and being a better father. I guess when I do socialize, it is at tattoo conventions where I can connect with people more like myself."

The combination of beauty and horror mark Joshua's best work.

Joshua sometimes finds himself frustrated when dealing with the business end of running his shop, but he tries to keep the challenges all in perspective. He says, "It is really difficult to balance the creative and the business side of tattooing. It kind of comes down to a right-brain-vs.-left-brain fight.

"It is frustrating when I'm in a super creative mode, sketching up my next piece, but I have to go deal with the phone book guy waiting in the lobby. And on top of that, there are apprentices to deal with, and then the customer who wants every possible element included into a tattoo the size of a dime. It can keep your days pretty interesting. I just try to take things one step at a time and to remember that at the end of the day, it's the art that counts."

A lotus flower.

133

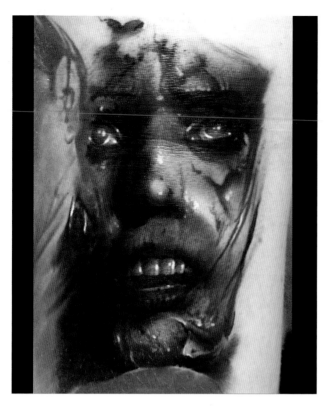

A horror face.

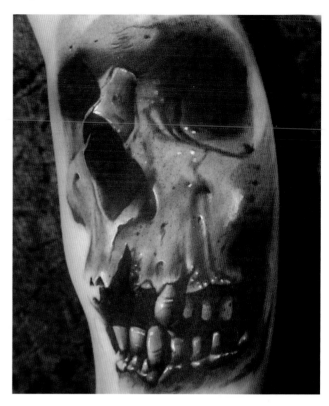

A hyper realistic take on a tattoo classic.

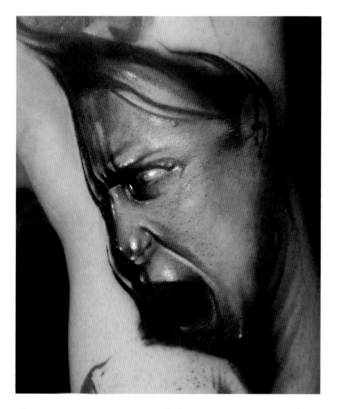

Interesting perspective and placement.

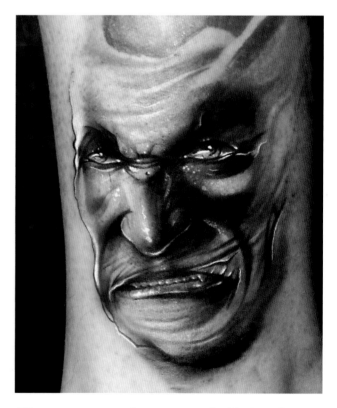

The green eyes stand out against the black and gray background.

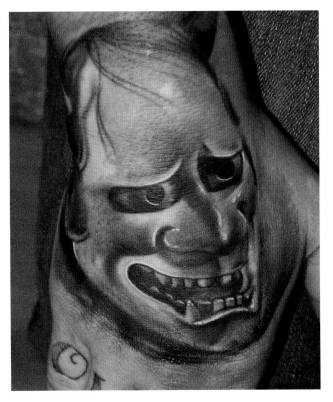

Black and gray Hanya mask.

Notice the highlights in this portrait.

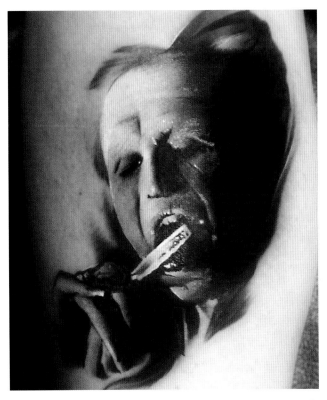

Joshua captures an impression of detail with painterly touches in this small tattoo.

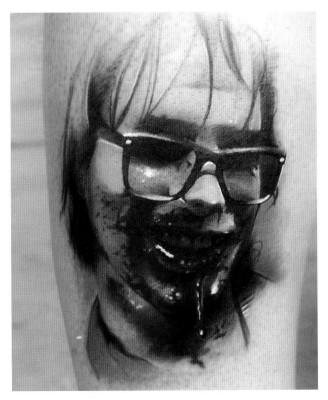

Blood and gore.

Joshua uses white lines to add bold highlights.

Oil painting by Joshua Carlton.

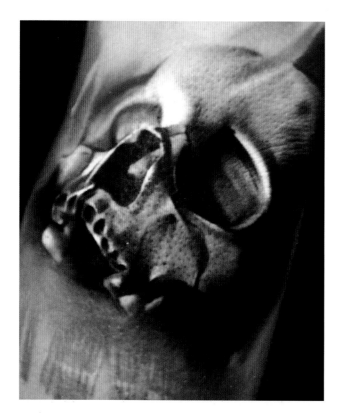
Joshua's take on the classic tattoo skull.

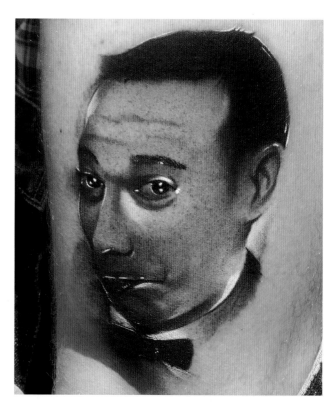
Pee Wee Herman

An oil painting by Joshua Carlton.

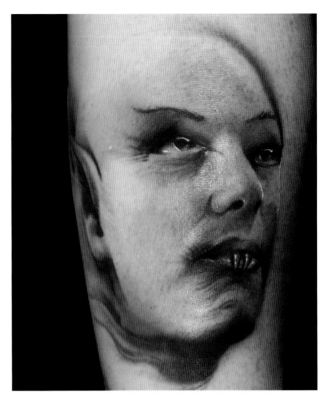

A vampire.

A Marilyn Manson tribute piece.

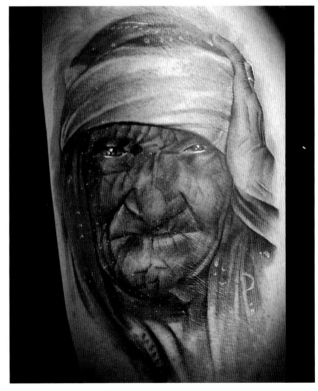

Joshua's technical mastery is apparent in the contrasting textural impressions.

A vampire.

In His Own Words: Joshua Carlton Q&A

Q: How long have you been tattooing?

A: Wow. It is hard to believe it, but I am now in my 18th year of tattooing.

Q: Do you remember anything about the first tattoo you ever did?

A: Actually, yes. It's on me. It is a moon with flames around it. It looks as bad today as the day I did it, but I will never cover it up. It is a constant reminder of how hard work pays off.

Q: Tell us a little bit about your style.

A: I've always remained pretty focused on realism. It is really where my heart is. I am an extreme realist, even to the point that I can't really think any other way. I would not make a great traditional artist, but I have a lot of respect for those guys. It takes a certain kind of thinking to pull that style off, and I can't do it. My goal has always been to find out how far I can take tattooing to make it look as believable as possible.

Q: Who are some of your influences, either tattooing or otherwise?

A: Michelangelo has always been my greatest influence in art. I have always had a tendency to be attracted to darker imagery, so as soon as I discovered the artwork of Paul Booth, it was love at first sight. Other early influences were Brian Everett, Jack Rudy, and Cap Szumski. I really do try to do my own thing,

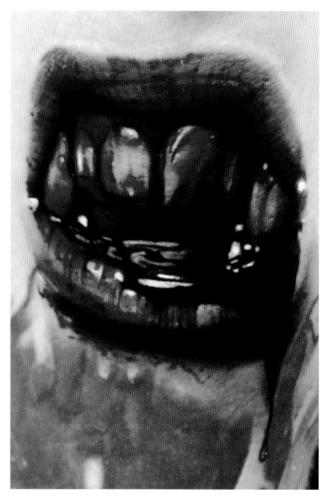

Vampire teeth.

but we all have our influences, and I find myself studying Spain's Robert Hernandez quite a bit. I make it a point to study more than just tattoo artists, but artists in general, living or dead. There is so much art out there to inspire us; it would be silly not to take advantage of all forms of it.

Q: *What do you do when you aren't tattooing?*

A: Tattooing really does tend to take over your life. When I'm not tattooing, I find myself thinking about tattooing. I like to go to bookstores with my family for relaxation. We are all avid readers, and I also like perusing the magazines. You never know what may spark an idea for a new piece.

I have always wanted to be more of an outdoorsy person. My wife and I took a trip to

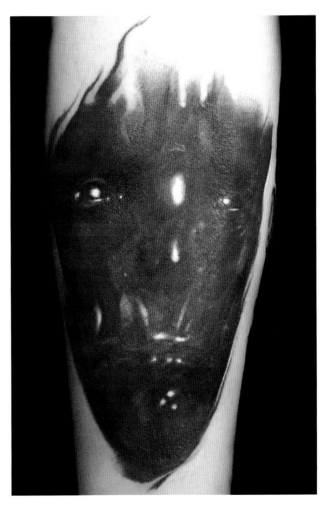

Portrait in red.

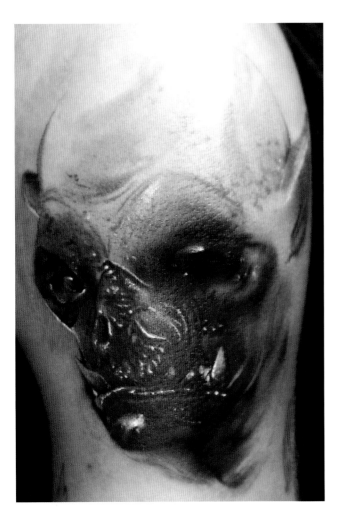

Creepy creature with disconcertingly realistic features.

Mammoth Cave a little while back, and we tried our hand at snowboarding last winter. I didn't find myself thinking about tattooing too much in those moments. I would definitely like to try more things outside of tattooing, but it is just hard to find the time.

Q: *Describe the tattoo scene in Shelbyville.*

A: Amazingly, Shelbyville was very receptive to us when we moved here. There is a large population of young people, 18-25 year-olds, and they quickly became interested in getting great tattoos once we moved into town. At first, we were concerned that the local community would not embrace a full custom shop with no flash, but it took no time at all for all of our artists to be booked for several weeks in advance.

139

A bat.

would have fire, one would have poisonous snakes, and the third would have that client waiting at the bottom! I had him as a client for a long time, until my wife and I moved to Arizona. And even when we were there, he would try to contact me from time to time!

Q: *Do you have a most memorable client or a funny tattoo that stands out?*

A: I have enough stories to fill your book! There have been so many through the years…I recently had a girl ask me if I would tattoo a vagina with teeth on her. That was pretty notable. A few years back, I had a client who would call me drunk after every appointment and tell me how good I was. He was always trying to bring me dinner or something. Most mornings, he would be in the shop parking lot waiting as I pulled in to open up, even if he didn't have an appointment. A close friend of mine used to joke about him and say that we should have three hidden chutes in front of the counter lobby for mouthy customers. One

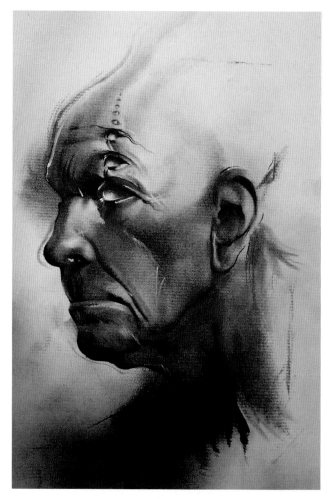

A charcoal sketch by Joshua Carlton.

140

A lady with a fan.

This is a unique take on the classic tattoo demon.

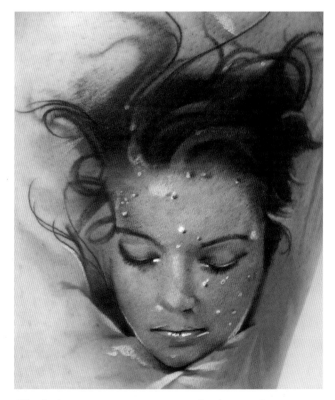

The hair serves as a contrasting background.

The eyes appear to glow in this portrait.

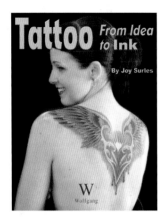

Tattoo - from Idea to Ink

Tattoo - From Idea To Ink traces the origin of a tattoo from its initial inception through the process of design and finally implementation in the hands of talented artists like Amanda Wachob of Blue Moon Tattoo in Buffalo, New York. With an abundance of colorful images and insightful text, this book provides a first-hand look at the stages a custom client experiences in getting the tattoo of his or her dreams. From understanding this process and reviewing the different styles of art available, *Tattoo - From Idea to Ink*, offers artwork, artists, and suggestions for anyone looking for that perfect piece of art. In addition to a full section filled with original artwork from master tattooists, the book features work by industry legends like Brandon Bond, Sarah Peacock, Zsolt Sarkozi, Shannon Schober, Mario Desa, Corey Rogers, Josh Woods, Nate Beavers, and many more.

Eleven Chapters   144 Pages $27.95   Over 400 photos, 100% color

Tattoo Bible

Whether you are preparing for your first tattoo or your twenty-seventh, you need artwork and designs that are just-right. *Tattoo Bible*, authored by Superior Tattoo, provides well over 500 pieces of unique flash art - flash never before compiled into one single book.

While most tattoo books available today concentrate on one specific genre, this *Tattoo Bible* covers many different genres and the ideas are endless.

This is not just a book to add to your collection - this is your collection. You can combine different pieces of art from within the book, or just take them as is. This book is for you and your imagination to do with as you wish.

Published by ArtKulture, an imprint of Wolfgang Publications, with images that are both striking and very useful to both the tattoo shop, and the tattoo aficionado.

Eleven Chapters   144 Pages $27.95   Over 500 photos, 100% color

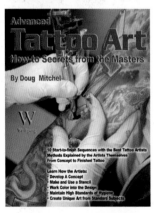

Advanced Tattoo Art

The art of the tattoo has emerged from the garage to the parlor, from the local bar to the boardroom. With interest in tattoos at a high point, the time is right for a detailed look at the art, and the artists, who create the elaborate designs.

Doug Mitchel take the reader inside the shops of ten well-known and very experienced artists spread across the country. Both a how-to book and a photo-intense look the world or tattoos; *Tattoo Art* includes interviews with the artists that explain not only how they do what they do, but also their personal preference for materials and methods. Detailed photo sequences follow each artist through a tattoo project. From customer concept, to sketch, outline, and the finished colorful design. The chapters document not only the techniques, but also the inks and tools used during each step of the process

Ten Chapters   144 Pages $27.95   Over 400 photos, 100% color

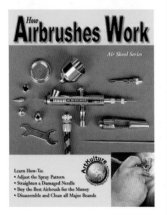

How Airbrushes Work

How Airbrushes Work is a comprehensive look at airbrush use, maintenance and repair. The book begins with a brief look at airbrush history, then moves to a discussion of the various airbrush types. This new book from ArtKulture, an imprint of Wolfgang Publications explains how to disassemble, clean and repair all the major brands. Even the best airbrush in the world isn't any good without a source of air. Steve discusses different compressor types and the advantages or disadvantages of each. Two chapters explain airbrush painting basics, Steve closes the book with a gallery of airbrush art, and an airbrush buyer's guide to help readers choose wisely when they buy their first, or their fifth, airbrush.

Available spring of 2009.

Ten Chapters   144 Pages $27.95   Over 500 photos, 100% color

PAINT EXPERT

How Airbrushes Work	$27.95
Air Brushing 101	$27.95
Adv. Custom Motorcycle Painting	$27.95
Advanced Airbrush Art	$27.95
Advanced Custom Painting Techniques	$27.95
Advanced Custom Painting Techniques (Spanish)	$27.95
Advanced Pinstripe Art	$27.95
Kustom Painting Secrets	$19.95
Custom Paint & Graphics	$27.95
Pro Airbrush Techniques	$27.95
How to Paint Barns & Buildings	$27.95

BIKER BASICS

Sheet Metal Fabrication	$27.95
How to FIX American V-Twin MC	$27.95

HOP-UP EXPERT

How to Hop & Customize your Bagger	$27.95
How to Hop & Customize your Softail	$27.95
How to Customize Your Star	$27.95

CUSTOM BUILDER SERIES

Adv Custom Motorcycle Wiring	$27.95
Adv Custom Motorcycle Assembly & Fabrication	$27.95
Adv. Custom Motorcycle Chassis	$27.95
How to Build a Cheap Chopper	$27.95
How to Build a Chopper	$27.95

SHEET METAL

Advanced Sheet Metal Fabrication	$27.95
Ultimate Sheet Metal Fabrication	$19.95

OLD SKOOL SKILLS

Barris: Grilles, Scoops, Fins and Frenching (Vol. 2)	$24.95
Barris: Flames Scallops, Paneling and Striping (Vol. 4)	$24.95

HOT ROD BASICS

How to Air Condition Your Hot Rod	$27.95
How to Chop Tops	$24.95
How to Wire your Hot Rod	$27.95

MOTORCYCLE RESTORATION SERIES

Triumph Resotoration	$29.95
Triumph MC Restoration Pre-Unit	$29.95

ILLUSTRATED HISTORY

Triumph Motorcycles	$32.95

HOME SHOP

How to Paint Tractors & Trucks	$27.95

TATTOO U Series

Tattoo Bible	$27.95
Tattoos Behind the Needle	$27.95
Tattoo- From Idea to Ink	$27.95
Advanced Tattoo Art	$27.95
Body Painting	$27.95

COMPOSITE GARAGE

Composite Materials	$27.95

Conclusion

People began adorning their bodies with tattoos more than 5,000 years ago, and we have come a long way in the development of the art. From the first etchings on skin in the Bronze Age to the hyper-realistic and abstract effects today's artists create, we might believe we have achieved the limits of tattoo artistry. However, by following the changes that have occurred in styles and techniques of just the artists in this book through their short careers, it becomes clear that we are still in an era of change, growth, and re-invention for tattooing. Each year, new technology in inks, machines, power supplies, and other technical aspects of the trade promise to continue to propel the artistry ever further. Meanwhile, tattooists continue to invigorate one another through a kind of healthy creative competition.

Through the ever-growing number of tattoo conventions to the profusion of videos, books, magazines, and other material, artists share information with one another in an industry that was once marked by secrecy. This increased openness, perhaps, has helped promote this evolution in the art as well as the inevitable development that takes place in any art form. The transition from cave scrawls to the flat, one-dimensional images of the Middle Ages parallels the movement of tattoo art from the ancient tribal to the Traditional styles; the increased realism in perspective and three-dimensionality that marked the Renaissance in painting, similarly, reflects the developments in tattoo art over the last 10 years. Artists who conscientiously position tattoo art among the fine arts are likely to be the visionaries who determine the direction of tattooing into the future.

The progression of tattoo art will continue onward and upward, with no end in sight. It is an exciting time to be a part of this world.

Artist Information

Brandon Bond ~ All or Nothing Tattoo
2569 S. Cobb Dr., Smyrna, GA 30080
www.AllorNothingTattoo.com
(770) 435-9966

Sunny Buick
www.SunnyBuick.com

Joshua Carlton ~ The Great American Tattoo Co.
5 Public Square, Indianapolis, IN 46176
www.JoshuaCarlton.com
(317) 398-8895

Matt Griffith~ 2 Dollar Pistol Tattoo
203 N. Bridge St., Chillicothe, OH 45601
www.ArtworkVigilante.com
(740) 772-2552

Dan Henk
www.DanHenk.com

Sean Herman ~ Royal Street Tattoo
110 N. Royal Street , Mobile, AL 36602
www.SeanHerman.com

Shannon Schober ~ Vitality Tattoo
1240 Brevard Rd. Suite #1, Asheville, NC 28806
www.VitalityTattoo.com
(828) 667-4344

Chris Thomas ~ Golden Lotus Tattoo
3901 E. Kiehl Ave. #D, Sherwood, AR 72120
www.GoldenLotusTattoos.com
(501) 834-6955

Amanda Wachob ~ Dare Devil Tattoo
174 Ludlow St., New York, NY
www.DareDevilTattoo.com
www.AmandaWachob.com
(212) 533-8303

John Wayne ~ Beesting Tattoo
348 South St., Belle River, Ontario, Canada
www.BeestingTattoo.com
(519) 728-4824